# COMMON GROUND

# COMMON GROUND

## MULTIFAMILY HOUSING IN LOS ANGELES

*Frances Anderton*

ANGEL CITY PRESS

Overleaf: The Courtyard at La Brea, 2014,
designed by Tighe Architecture and John V. Mutlow Architects.
This page: A party at the Edward Fickett-designed Hollywood Riviera.

In loving memory of two brilliant people who taught me to see the beauty and life in buildings: my friend, John Chase, and my father, Sam Anderton.

# Contents

Opposite: The wood-clad Pico Eleven, 2018, by KFA Architects, sits on a busy arterial, but tenants share a serene environment on the rooftop deck.

"No one moves to Los Angeles to get an apartment. Or at least not to end up in one," Robert Greene wrote in *LA Weekly* in 2005, when apartment construction was exploding in Los Angeles. No one—except millions of Angelenos, including yours truly. When I arrived in L.A. thirty years ago, I moved into a six-unit apartment building in Santa Monica: Hillcrest Apartments.

The building came with a pedigree. It was designed by Frank Gehry in 1962, in collaboration with Fereydoon Ghaffari—Gehry's former classmate at USC and colleague at the office of architect and planner Victor Gruen. Gehry and Ghaffari lived there at one time, as did their friends and family members. Friends of Gehry's included Ernest Fleischmann, the onetime director of the Los Angeles Philharmonic; the artist Judy Chicago; Milton Wexler, Gehry's famed psychoanalyst; and Gehry's sister, Doreen Gehry Nelson. Gehry took up residence with his wife Berta Aguilera and their son, Alejandro, and connected two units. There is little about the building, however, that

foretells Gehry's future architectural adventurousness. It is understated, a white-stuccoed, U-shaped structure wrapped around a small common area, raised over parking at back and front. It has gabled overhangs above balconies with chunky wood railings, which give it a hint of Japanese design. Gehry intended Hillcrest to fit with the craftsman bungalows in the Ocean Park neighborhood.

But there were hints of unconventionality, argued Gehry's biographer, Paul Goldberger. Those balustrades were set "slightly in front of . . . and extend below [the deck] . . . creating a strong pattern of vertical lines"; a cube projecting beyond the wall on the upper level, and recessed doors on the right front that offset the "mass of the chimney," combine to make, writes Goldberger, "a subtle asymmetrical arrangement of solids and voids."

The "solids and voids" on the exterior are the outward expression of interior space—and organizing space, says Nelson, is her brother's innate gift. "He has perfect pitch, spatially." It turned out that behind the unprepossessing façade lay six well-planned dwellings. Kitchens and dining and living areas flow smoothly from one to the other. They are bathed in natural light

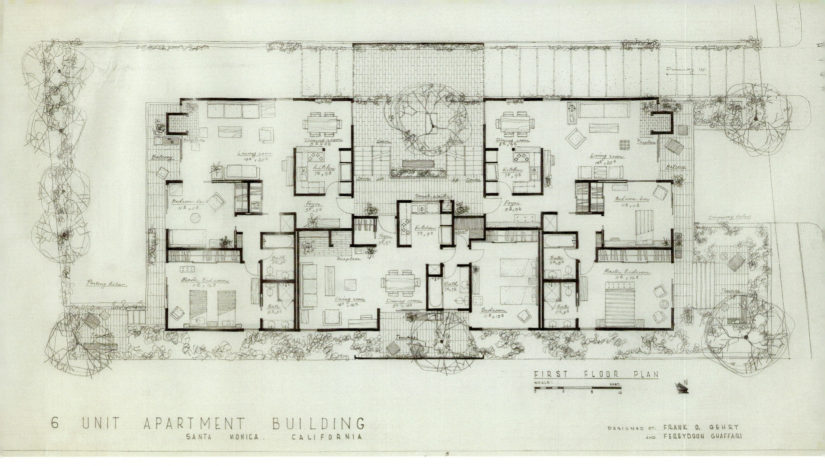

**Hillcrest Apartments, first-floor plan**

and cooled with flowing air that is delivered in a daily dance from multiple aspects: tall, slender panes, regular and jalousie windows, high clerestories, sliding patio doors, and, upstairs, skylights over entrance lobbies. Fireplaces and desks are built into alcoves. Details like a skirting board and continuous wooden picture rail add a sense of proportion and height to regular eight-foot ceilings, along with an invitation to hang art. There is a sense of spaciousness but no extraneous space. Nelson praised the economy of her flat at the top front of the building, especially the small, efficient kitchen (located in the cube that extends from the top floor), in which everything was reachable from one spot. "My brother does great kitchens," she says. "I was married to an art

dealer, and we had huge parties and we could grind out meals from that room." Of course, clarifies Nelson, kitchens are only a small expression of her brother's "all-encompassing genius."

Genius notwithstanding, few of its residents stayed very long. Many were there for a brief hiatus, post-divorce. Gehry's friends all moved on, conforming to Greene's assertion that Angelenos do not stay in apartments. "An apartment here is a way-station," he explained, "a temporary fix until the college loans are paid off, or until the band is signed, or the screenplay is sold, or you make partner, or you tie the knot." In my case, I did not budge. I got the keys in 1991 and woke up in 2021 to find I had lived in the same apartment

Hillcrest Apartments, interior. Slender windows punching through a picture rail bring sophistication.

building for three decades. This has given me a sense of failure, for not having become a home-owning Angeleno, but on reflection I realized I had never really felt a desire to move.

I had considered doing so at various points. Ten years in, my boyfriend moved in, and then came a daughter, and we were squeezed for space in my seven-hundred-square-foot, one-bedroom unit upstairs. We looked around at homes for sale in more affordable areas, but wound up choosing to move to the two-bedroom apartment downstairs, once occupied by Wexler.

In addition to the liveable interiors, the building is attractive socially. Apartments are arranged around the court and reached by shared, external staircases that cause residents to run into each other, creating a sense of community; we are there for each other when we need anything, from receiving parcels to watching each other's children and sometimes dining together. During the years I lived by myself, I felt safe, tucked between neighbors; later, our only child grew up in a building where she never felt alone. But the neighborliness is not oppressive, because each unit also has its own private balcony or deck, shaded by pepper and eucalyptus trees. Gehry says he wanted the building to provide a sense of "peripheral connection," a subtle, reassuring human presence, so residents could be "communal with the other people in the building without infringing on their privacy, or they on yours."

Admittedly, there were other reasons to stay: stable rent, and a walkable, pleasant neighborhood (filled with an array of interesting multifamily buildings) with good public schools. But socially and aesthetically, this place afforded a very good life.

Perhaps I was primed to enjoy it. What constitutes home is doubtless influenced by the dwellings that shaped us, and in my case I spent much of my childhood and early adulthood in England, living in apartments, typically in Georgian or Victorian row houses subdivided into flats. I liked the beehive-like nature of these stacked dwellings, but they could be dark and feel cramped, due to their single-aspect windows and lack of flow into shared open space. However, my architecture-mad father stacked our shelves with books about early modernist housing, featuring schemes for future living by the likes of Le Corbusier, Walter Gropius, and Richard Neutra: open-plan flats with plentiful sunlight and glass doors leading to decks and balconies. I imbibed this imagery and aspired to this lifestyle. Later, I encountered a different kind of housing on a trip to Jaipur, India: the *haveli*, a courtyard townhouse. Several floors surround private inner courts, with a fringe of storefronts for local businesses at the base, facing outward to the street. Higher floors, focused onto the courts, were exclusively for extended family members. The roofs were for relaxation, and for viewing other townspeople on the roofs of their courtyard buildings, which were built side-by-side, multiplying like cells into the larger organism of a city. This mode of living was replicated in varied forms in China, the Islamic world, and in parts of the Mediterranean, and was the opposite of the rowhouse living I was used to, which tipped occupants from the front door directly onto the street. It piqued an interest in housing as a self-contained community, and in the court and rooftop as social spaces.

Shared stairways bring residents together at Hillcrest Apartments.

On returning from Jaipur, I joined the editorial staff of the *Architectural Review*. Reyner Banham, author of the famed book *Los Angeles: The Architecture of Four Ecologies*, had been a writer at the *AR,* and the magazine hewed to a philosophy that my editor-in-chief Peter Davey termed "modernism with a human face." My first assignment was to visit the West Coast and report on the cheerfully subversive, formally experimental design by the likes of Gehry, Morphosis, and Eric Owen Moss. Four years later, I moved to Los Angeles and found, in this mecca for single-family homes, my dream apartment.

Not all apartments in L.A. are dreamy by any stretch: thousands are poorly designed or situated, and offer no rental stability. Obviously, living cheek by jowl can present challenges as well as joys. To paraphrase Jean-Paul Sartre, hell can be other people, especially when they live on the other side of a cheap, thin wall. But a surprising number of multifamily buildings offer Angelenos their own version of this domestic dream: connected dwellings that combine privacy with

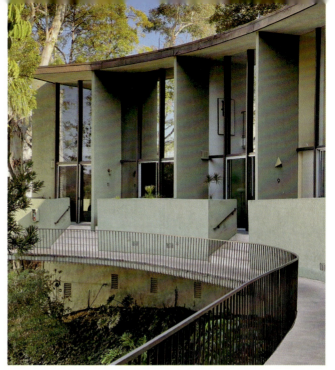

Ray Kappe designed 3625 Fredonia Drive, 1964, in Studio City.

Residents enjoy their own patios and a shared, sweeping walkway.

sociability, make the most of the Southern California sun, and connect to the great outdoors. Some are large, grand in their design. Many are very modest. Some bring people together around a court or green space, others through shared amenities such as laundries and gyms. Some are full of architectural character and have evocative names: Village Green, Hollywood Riviera, Chase Knolls, Treehouse, St. Elmo Village. Most are simply street addresses, with mailboxes bearing an impersonal list of unit numbers or letters. But behind those numbers and letters are people, co-existing in micro-communities that offer residents a sense of place and human connection in a vast, sprawling megalopolis. "Worlds within worlds" is how Rohan Silva describes these places. Silva is the founder of Second Home, a coworking and cultural venue, and he lives at Atwater Bungalows—a compound of Pueblo-style dwellings on rolling slopes in Echo Park, designed in the 1920s by Robert Stacy-Judd, an ardent aficionado of Mayan and Aztec architecture,

for a dentist named Dr. H. Gale Atwater. The place is both a Meso-American stage set and a place to call home, where neighbors are "always in and out of each other's houses, borrowing odds and ends," says Silva. These worlds within worlds can be as fantastical as Atwater Bungalows. They can take the form of humble bungalow courts or lavish apartment-hotels; peaceful garden apartments, architecturally ambitious affordable housing, and twenty-first-century lofts on arterials with rooftop pools and the amenities you would expect in a boutique hotel. Some of these dwellings were designed by unknown builders and designers, others by high-profile architects or developers who put as much of their soul into creating great multifamily buildings as they did into experimental houses.

Despite its many charms, however, such housing is widely perceived as a poor relation to the proper mode of living: in a detached house. With the exception of hyper-urban New York, America has a hierarchy of dwellings, topped by the single-family, owner-occupied

Rudolph Schindler's 1949 Laurelwood Apartments in Studio City fuse the California courtyard with modernism.

house with a yard and a car. This is the incarnation of what Banham has described as "the dream of the urban homestead" and "the country-house culture of the fathers of the U.S. Constitution." Los Angeles, he continued in his 1971 book, "cradles and embodies the most potent current version of the great bourgeois vision of the good life in a tamed countryside." Even though both houses and apartments are the products of rampant real estate speculation, the house is perceived as more of a "home," an ideal undergirded by land-use policy, tax benefits, and popular culture that have crystallized over a century and diminished other forms of dwellings. In fact, Todd Gish, an architect and urban designer, points out in a masterful dissertation about the early development of multifamily dwellings in L.A. that, starting in the early twentieth century, flats and apartments were not even called "homes." In a December 1921 issue of *Los Angeles Realtor*, reports Gish, readers were told that the word "home," as used by the (United States) Department of Commerce, applies only to dwellings occupied by a single family; the presumption was that apartment living—at least for those with options—was a temporary stage for the young until it came "time to select the district, type, and style of dwelling they ultimately will require." This

bias was reinforced by zoning—more than two-thirds of residential land in L.A. is designated for single-family homes and duplexes. Their appeal has been elevated by the design industries—legions of architects and interior and landscape designers are kept busy creating dream homes—and disseminated worldwide by shelter magazines, style sections of newspapers, and now social media. Hollywood adds to the allure with fictional depictions of domesticity in Los Angeles, in which, invariably, families and rich people live in houses while criminals, singles, and poor people live in apartments. Few are the TV shows that glamorize connected living in Los Angeles, though a famous exception is *Melrose Place*, the soap opera set in a Spanish-style courtyard and unforgettable to anyone who came of age in the 1990s. Even *Melrose Place*, however, supported the old assumption about living in an apartment: it was temporary. Since there was no one over the age of thirty on the show, one assumed the oversexed denizens of *Melrose Place* were destined to move on, doubtless to a large house in 90210.

Generally, multifamily living, especially connected apartments—a party wall, *quelle horreur!*—occupies a second tier, a fact that became especially personal when our daughter was old enough to bring schoolmates home. Most of her close buddies lived in houses, and she felt so embarrassed by her apartment that she would try to avoid having friends visit. As she became a teenager, however, she was astonished to discover that her pals liked her home. This was partly because my husband filled the place with vinyl and cool posters, but perhaps they also appreciated the very same qualities that we did: its coziness, coupled with its openness, its connection to the outside, and its neighborliness. The California house has been so exalted that it may come as a surprise that the construction of multifamily housing at times equaled single family residential development in the region's early days. Gish writes that by one count in the mid-1920s, nearly half of the city's 328,000 dwelling units were in duplexes and apartment buildings. More building permits were issued for multifamily than single-family homes during another boom in the mid-1950s, according to architectural historian Steven A. Treffers. Now apartment construction is ascendant again in Los Angeles, and is reshaping the cityscape as well as the options for domestic life. By some reports, by early 2020, there were approximately 500,000 single-family homes in the city of Los Angeles, and more than 600,000 apartments spread across 118,000 properties. As of this writing, the majority of residential buildings under construction in L.A. County are multi-unit buildings or Accessory Dwelling Units (ADUs), one- or two-story small dwellings also known as granny flats, added to the backyards of single family homes. We have reached a point in the Southland where the single-family home is outdated. It gobbles up land and resources; it is financially out of reach for most young—and older—people; and it does not meet the needs of growing numbers of Angelenos who do not fit the nuclear family model. Furthermore, it fails to address an urgent demand for housing in a region with thousands of people living on the streets. For the majority in Los Angeles, home ownership has become more of a dream than a reality, and they must choose between leaving the city to buy a house or remain in L.A. in some form of multifamily dwelling.

Despite the dominance of multifamily housing, it seems to be perpetually treated as the problem child; even affordable housing projects demanded by voters to alleviate homelessness invariably face pushback from neighbors once a specific site is determined. The

**The architect Lorcan O'Herlihy (LOHA) describes Westgate1515 as an "urban village."**

Sierra Bonita Affordable Housing, 2012, designed by Tighe Architecture for West Hollywood Community Housing, is ornamented with laser-cut metalwork.

prospect of increased traffic is almost always a concern, but perhaps it would be less of a political problem if people valued apartment living, or better yet, desired it. *Common Ground* celebrates the best of it, demonstrating that multifamily housing is not second tier, that it can take top honors by other measures of domestic pleasure, and that it is integral to the life of the city and—when equitable and well-designed—offers in itself an aspirational experience. This proposition was modeled very effectively in 2020 when Christopher Hawthorne, the city of L.A.'s chief design officer, invited architects and landscape architects to participate in a design competition called Low-Rise: Housing Ideas for Los Angeles. This challenge, he explained, was "to help us imagine appealing and sustainable new models of low-rise, multi-unit housing" for middle-income Angelenos—those who are unable to pay today's house prices or market-rate rents yet earning enough to be ineligible for subsidized, or "affordable" housing. It was ambitious in scope, essentially asking

entrants to design their way around the constraints that have shaped home in L.A., from parking rules to the politics of housing. The resulting concepts were aimed at showing homeowners in single-family neighborhoods that somewhat denser housing in their communities could bring a host of benefits: well-designed, sustainable dwellings offering opportunities for intergenerational or more socially connected living, along with a redistribution of equity, and greater vitality to suburban areas in all corners of the city. Hawthorne's goal was soft diplomacy; to rally people around what has been referred to as "gentle density" in anticipation of Senate Bills 9 and 10 (passed in 2021) that would allow between two and ten new dwellings to be added to a single family lot. While the "challenge" produced an abundance of terrific new designs submitted by designers from all over the world, many of its lessons were already on display, in the many marvels of multifamily design in the hills and flatlands of Los Angeles, dating back more than a century.

"L.A.'s multifamily housing is a huge subject that has been ignored and overlooked," says Alan Hess, historian of California architecture, adding, "Innovations in multifamily architecture have been as great as those in the single-family house that gets all the attention." Those innovations include many configurations of courtyard housing as well as the garden apartments for low-income residents on superblocks, built by an optimistic public housing authority during the New Deal years, and swank apartment buildings offering the amenities of motels and hotels. For more than a century, builders and designers have experimented with interior layouts, with ways to incorporate the car, and with new materials and architectural styles. They have synthesized Los Angeles's relaxed, open lifestyle in a balmy climate with housing typologies borrowed from the region's pre-Columbian past, from the Mediterranean and from twentieth-century modernism.

It is here, for example, that the designer-builder couple Arthur and Nina Zwebell and the brothers Walter S. and F. Pierpont Davis took the courtyard house of Southern Spain and recast it as a romantic backdrop for Hollywood starlets to lead louche lives in the 1920s, complete with space at the back to park the Ford Model T. Here also, Irving Gill, Rudolph Schindler, and Richard Neutra fused the radical experiments with open-space planning and industrial materials—which were taking place in interwar Europe—with the easy access to the outside of Southland living, sprinkled on Southern California light, and created some of the most delightful small, connected housing in the history of twentieth-century modernist architecture. Today, imaginative developers and architects are creating housing for the affluent and for the formerly unhoused that offers a new kind of multifamily lifestyle: lifted high off the ground, with outdoor decks, roofs, and bridges to gather on and take in the purple sunset. They show that very large apartment buildings—of which many are appearing on the region's arterials, often characterless and lumpen—can have the verve of their predecessors, although laser-cut, digitally designed metalwork may replace the decorative wrought iron railings, gates, and balustrades of the period revival courts; the smooth stucco of the early moderns may have been replaced by vivid-colored Hardie Board; and the abundant greenery of the ideal California yard now climbs walls and takes root—somewhat surreally—in deep planters on rooftop terraces several floors above the dirt. Meanwhile, a new generation of designers is cutting its teeth on low-density group living, which has returned in the form of backyard housing on single-family lots. This is pushing innovation in both the formal design of petite dwellings and their process of construction. A combination of exorbitant building costs and computerization that makes it possible to custom-order online—and then manufacture most elements of a home offsite—have birthed modular and prefab container homes, decked out in sleek wood and laminates and offered up as ideal homes for mom-in-law to grow old in while caring for the grandkids living in the main house.

There has been some wonderful research by scholars and journalists on aspects of multifamily dwellings in Los Angeles, and it supports much of the narrative in this book. A bibliography provides a wealth of information on further reading. I also learned a lot about the topic in my past work at KCRW, the National Public Radio affiliate in Santa Monica, where I served first as producer for Warren Olney's current affairs shows *Which Way, L.A.?* and *To the Point*, and then as host of a radio show called *DnA: Design and Architecture*. From *Which Way, L.A.?* I learned about the forces that had shaped the Southland, often involving

St. Elmo Village

conflict over power, race, and land, themes that converge in housing. At *DnA*, I watched as designers navigated these tensions, reinvigorating the form and shape of the Cityscape of Angels. As the years passed and a moribund downtown revived and a mass transit system reemerged, it became evident that multifamily building construction was exploding—in unexpected places like arterial streets and by freeways—while access to the single-family house was shrinking. So in 2019, I embarked, with producer Avishay Artsy, on a series of stories called *This Is Home in LA*. The series went on for weeks because there was simply no end to the types of housing people lived in, from boats in Marina Del Rey, to apartments above Starbucks in newly minted downtown Playa Vista, to condos with panoramic views in all-glass towers by freeways in downtown. And in each kind of home, I met people who simply would not want to live anywhere else. It became resoundingly clear that the single-family house, so long the defining dwelling for Los Angeles, held an outsize place in the imagination.

There are thousands of apartments in Los Angeles, and the taxonomy of building types is long. This is not an encyclopedic study of all of them. Rather, I am putting a spotlight on a slice of those that are intentionally centered on shared space outdoors and shared amenities, starting in the 19-teens when the bungalow court and the serviced apartment-hotel took off, both offering instant community to newcomers in the region, along with the pleasures of the Los Angeles landscape. The journey takes in courtyard housing in styles both historicist and modernist: the visionary garden apartments of the New Deal era, Googie-inspired postwar apartment living, mid-rise contemporary courtyard housing for low- and high-income residents, hotel-inspired loft living in new and retrofitted structures, and ADUs and the new era of low-rise backyard housing. While most of the buildings shown are pivotal—exemplars of a type, often designed by professional architects—I have also included some by talented, and under-recognized, commercial apartment designers, like Sam Reisbord. In addition, I have highlighted some unique communities created by individuals with a vision, like St. Elmo Village, a hub of visual arts and community activism founded by two artists, Rozzell Sykes and his nephew, Roderick Sykes, and L.A. Eco-Village, a cooperative founded on ideas about living more sustainably under the driving force of Lois Arkin.

You cannot examine multifamily housing in Los Angeles without considering the context of zoning and lending practices that have divided people by race, class, and type of home. Redlining, racially restrictive covenants, the forming of single-family (or R1) zones, and the downzoning of neighborhoods with a lively mix of single and multifamily housing types, have caused deep urban segregation while stimulating disdain for

multifamily living and, in the opinion of many experts, sending up the cost of housing generally. "Housing in L.A. is terribly expensive, because for years we haven't been building enough," says Frederick Zimmerman, professor of public health and of urban planning at UCLA. "We haven't been building enough because we have only so much land and we've down-zoned it to prevent multifamily housing, which was stigmatized—largely by white people—in part because of its association with people of color." In this book, I situate buildings in this framework but mostly I focus on the architectural design and the lived experience they offer their residents: How do they work as "homes"? Are they well-planned, with access to natural light, air, and greenery? Do they have architectural character? Do they provide a positive sense of connection? I have answers from people who made the buildings and the people who live in them, generously letting me visit and sharing their insights about what makes or breaks multifamily living. This narrative takes in the failures as well as the successes in aspirational apartment design.

After all, apartment living in L.A. is not always easy. For starters, it can be so pricey. Building real estate has

The rooftop terrace at Treehouse Hollywood

been L.A.'s raison d'être, its engine of growth, and yet there is never enough of it. Responsibility for building that housing lies mostly with private developers whose primary concern is making a return on their investment; they will build what they think the market will bear, not what the general population needs. Occupants can face the instability of losing their home to rent increases or eviction, along with other shortcomings of being a renter—no equity and lack of agency. Limitations on how to decorate an apartment or a ban on pets or rules against plants are subtle but constant reminders that the landlord is in control. But some enlightened developers and policymakers are starting to think about strengthening the financial foundations of rental living. So *Common Ground* also features some condominiums and explores some of the innovation in connected housing models that bridge renting and owning, including housing cooperatives, community land trusts, and even REITs (Real Estate Investment Trusts) that renters can invest in. The goal, says Max Levine—cofounder of the REIT called Nico (Neighborhood Investment Company), where renters at its Spicy Watermelon property were invited to help choose the plants for the common areas in addition to buying shares in the property—was "to elevate renting in a way that it's not viewed by people who are renters as being less than or inferior to the experience of homeownership." It becomes evident that creativity in financing can enhance the connection to place as much as a clever floor plan.

Researching *Common Ground* has entailed a joyful exploration of treasures hidden in plain sight. I have spent happy afternoons amidst the old growth trees and birdsong of Bowen Court in Pasadena and Village Green in Baldwin Hills. I've sat in the outdoor room on the roof of One Santa Fe, the quarter-mile-long block of rental housing over shops in the Arts District, and in the surreally lush garden atop Treehouse, a coliving

building in Hollywood. I have scouted Nickerson Downs, the postwar public housing complex in Watts that was designed by Paul R. Williams with the best of intentions in its time; and I've dined around the fire pit with the residents of the 3rd Street "compound" in Venice, a cluster of cottages in an Edenic garden created by a pair of benevolent landlords who chose to turn three unconnected lots into a self-contained community. The journey has been full of revelations, from learning about the byzantine complexity of getting thoughtful housing built to finding, repeatedly, that a highly desirable attribute in multifamily housing is a sense of containment, of being sequestered from the city outside, of living in a "world within a world."

I did most of the work on this book in 2021, during the COVID-19 pandemic quarantine. This was a time when thousands of people vacated newly urbanized city centers like downtown Los Angeles, desperate for a spacious home with an airy outdoor space. House prices shot up, and it looked for a while as if the burgeoning multifamily living trend might stall. As it turns out, for many, the "worlds within worlds" were a lifesaver. For Silva and his family at their complex in Echo Park, the little community became a pod. At Treehouse Hollywood, forty or so residents had each other for company and never felt the intense isolation experienced by people who were living alone during that time. Its co-creator Prophet Walker says they found ways to help each other, watching children or playing games online from their rooms, while social distancing measures kept the illness itself at bay. Later he reflected: "When you're in proximity and you know your neighbor, you can be supported by a neighbor."

To be clear, multifamily living worked during the pandemic when it delivered to its residents the COVID-era essentials: fresh air, access to the outside, indoor areas roomy enough for co-dwellers not to drive each other mad, and social spaces with enough room for social distancing. Just how much these attributes had become priorities rang out in the fall of 2021, when UC Santa Barbara released plans for a new student residence that proposed a warren of tiny sleeping areas with no natural light in a deep plan building. It boasted state-of-the-art artificial environmental design, including fake windows lit with LED bulbs—the kinds of techno-optimistic inventions that are often met with enthusiasm in California. Instead, a collective cry of horror went up. This was multi-unit living at its very worst. The pandemic had reordered priorities for decent, healthful, multifamily living space—much as the tuberculosis pandemic a century ago gave rise to healthful, airy houses and apartments in Los Angeles.

In recent years in Los Angeles there has been a lot of talk about the housing crisis, but less talk of the housing itself. I hope this book will inspire fellow apartment dwellers to take pride in the buildings they reside in, encourage housing historians to unearth many more multifamily gems, and emphasize to developers, designers, policymakers, and homeowners that connected living should never be seen as second-best—that it even can be an option for life, not an obligatory starter before the starter-home. The buildings you will see in these pages demonstrate that multifamily housing can be highly desirable—well-planned and full of character, with access to air, greenery, and personal outdoor space, and the reassuring presence of neighbors bumping into each other in shared, or "common" ground.

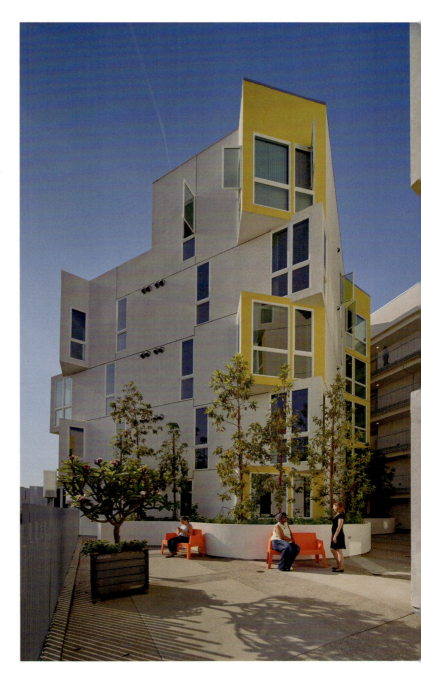

**Mosaic Gardens at Westlake, low-income units designed by Lahmon Architects for LINC Housing.**

The roof of Millennium Santa Monica, designed by Michael W. Folonis Architects, is a magnet for residents.

# 01

# MULTIFAMILY HOUSING AND THE CALIFORNIA DREAM

This story of common ground begins in Los Angeles in the early 1910s, an era that set the stage for the development of a uniquely Angeleno style of connected living. In far-off Europe, dark clouds were swelling, portending a horrendous war that would destroy old empires, empower America, and have profound consequences beyond the conflict, extending even to Los Angeles's residential design. But in the City of Angels, the sun was shining and optimism was in the air. Since the mid-1880s, city boosters had been aggressively selling a dream of a sun-kissed, orange-scented Eden to dissatisfied midwesterners fed up with cold winters and poor health. According to a blitz of colorful advertising, land was cheap and jobs were plentiful. Anything was possible in L.A. These PR efforts paid off in plenty, ushering in a rapidly growing population in the Southland and ambitious development projects. The Los Angeles Aqueduct, opened in 1913, had brought forth gushing water and, by extension, huge opportunities for growth

Opposite: The Bryson Apartment-Hotel on Wilshire Boulevard, built in 1913.

into the San Fernando Valley. People were pouring in by the thousands. They arrived daily on trains from the Midwest and the East, hoping to cure their tuberculosis, rampant in industrial cities, or get a fresh start—in oil, perhaps, or farming, or property development. Adventurous young people were seeking stardom in the extraordinary new movie industry taking off in Hollywood. Or they were tourists, simply taking some R and R away from harsh winters back home. This was all making the fledgling real estate lobby very happy indeed. Banks, merchants, housing, and transit builders had formed the Los Angeles Realty Board (LARB) in 1903 and were busy pushing the product that was then as plentiful as California oranges: undeveloped land. Newcomers rushed to buy empty plots in subdivisions, or lots with newly built cottages, and the city's population leapt from around 170,000 people in 1900 to over 500,000 in 1910, and more than 2.2 million by 1930. The rental business was also doing extremely well. Downtown Los Angeles was already chock-full of apartment buildings, and now they were spreading beyond its bounds. By 1910, the *Los Angeles Times* was advising property owners that the land in that area was too valuable for building mere single-family homes, notes historian Ruth Wallach.

From L.A.'s earliest days, great numbers of rental and multifamily dwellings were being built. Not that one might know it from the breathless boosterism. The single-family house was mythologized in the press and promotional copy about the city. The image of Los Angeles as a haven of owner-occupied houses in jasmine-scented yards—an endless garden city—was so persuasive that new arrivals "believed the promises that every man and woman could have a castle of their own," writes historian Wade Graham. The house was even considered morally superior to apartment buildings. When multi-unit rental structures first started appearing in the late 1800s, they "impressed many as scandalous in their implicitly promiscuous housing of unrelated strangers, men and women alike," wrote former California State Librarian Kevin Starr in the introduction to *Making a Better World: Public Housing, the Red Scare, and the Direction of Modern Los Angeles.* Ownership of a home, on the other hand, "implied personal maturity, a deeper stake in history, even a better moral condition, than that reached by renters."

People may have desired a house and "a better moral condition," but it was out of reach for most of them, because at the time prospective buyers had to provide a fifty-percent down payment and then pay off the mortgage in five to ten years. So all manner of new arrivals in L.A. had to rent a place to live. They had plenty of options. Newcomers could find a rental in the yard of a single-family house, because homeowners routinely added extra dwellings—like the modern Accessory Dwelling Units, or ADUs—in a practice known then as lot-packing. There were rooming houses in converted Victorian mansions and apartment buildings like those in older cities: two- to four-story

Bowen Court, soon after it opened in 1911.

brick structures with tenement-like flats. There were duplexes and a curious kind of dwelling known as a Four-Flat, or "apartment in disguise," a two-story period revival building with flats on either side of a central stair, that was designed to make passersby believe that it was a house. Then there were house courts: single lots jammed with one-story wood or tar paper shacks, packed with people and deemed "slums" by early reformers. There were also some attractive new options: the bungalow court and the apartment-hotel.

## Bowen Court and the Bungalow Court Boom

In 1911, two enterprising brothers, designer-speculators Arthur and Alfred Heineman, unveiled their latest creation at 539 East Villa Street in Pasadena: Bowen Court, twenty-three little cottages arranged in facing pairs on either side of an L-shaped central pathway

set off at a right angle to the road, like a mini-street. On the street was a streetcar line, dropping potential tenants right there. The cottages, which came in a mix of double and single units, had prominent porches and broad gable roofs, and distinct shingle and clapboard sidings. An orderly row of lamps marched down the path, which was lined with freshly planted palms. Facing the street edge was a low boundary wall in "peanut brittle" clinker (kiln-blackened) brick that was fashionable at the time. This was a bungalow court, and remains today as the earliest extant example in its original location in Pasadena. It is also the largest and most lavish. It cost $41,000 to build, almost as much as the Gamble House arts and crafts estate.

The bungalow court, recounts urban planner Laura Chase in her 1980 study "Gardens and Slums: House Courts and Bungalow Courts in Los Angeles, 1900–1930," was a clever amalgamation of the impoverished

Bowen Court, 2021

house court—of which there were thousands—and the classy bungalow, the woodsy, one-story house with porches and verandas set within a garden that was already so popular in Southern California. One of the first bungalow courts was Saint Francis Court in Pasadena, designed by Sylvanus Marston and built in 1909. The grouping of single or duplex cottages around a central garden or pathway, on a house lot, combined "the convenience and efficient land usage of the apartment with the garden atmosphere of the bungalow," writes Chase. Contrary to the bungalow, which enshrined hearty individualism in a suburban form, the bungalow court contained an urban, semi-public realm. The courts offered "privacy and at the same time community and fellowship," in the words of Juan Dela Cruz, an independent researcher at Pasadena Heritage, a historic preservation organization. Bungalow courts were built from 1909 to 1930 in most low and moderate income residential neighborhoods, says Chase. They were often located near transit lines and flourished in tourist-magnets like Santa Monica and Pasadena. While stylistically they ran the architectural gamut, the classic early bungalow courts featured detached cottages in the craftsman style of the detached bungalows, though the dwellings could be conjoined, with broad doors and windows, overhanging roofs, verandas, and porches with hanging baskets of flowers. Interiors featured carved wooden nooks, built-in bookcases, and tilework by artisans such as Pasadena's Ernest Batchelder.

Bowen Court was luxe, but bungalow courts were usually built cheaply out of wood frame and cladding, and they were a boon for builders, who could pack multiple dwellings on a single lot. *Architectural Record* admired them in a December 1913 issue for combining the efficient land use of an apartment without "introducing a brick wall where a view ought to be."

The open court was a practical device for bringing light and fresh air to each unit, and the complex provided instant community. Newlyweds and young families lived in the cottages. They suited seniors and singles, who were coming to L.A. in large numbers, and especially attracted women living alone. *Ladies Home Journal* wrote in an article titled "Community Idea for Women," that Bowen Court's cottages were "close enough together to afford a feeling of protection, but far enough apart to provide room for little grass plots between them." To emphasize the conviviality, Bowen Court even had a clubhouse, an artfully rustic and rumpled structure made of chunky, knotted logs with a thatched roof and a rubble-stone base, where people could take time to enjoy afternoon tea together.

The early bungalow courts were so popular that soon speculators took over and builders threw them up, from designs ordered from books of architectural plans. By 1913, nearly 10,000 people inhabited 621 courts in Los Angeles, says Todd Gish, a scholar of housing development; two years later, over 16,000 people lived in 1,202 courts. They became so ubiquitous that some people became jaded. In a 1916 issue of *House Beautiful* magazine, Pasadena resident Gertrude Appleton Luckey expressed weariness with the "constant repetition" in bungalow court design, writing that "one looks anxiously for something different, something with a touch of originality that will attract the eye without offending the taste." By repetition, presumably she was referring to the craftsman style. Luckey was quick to add that she was "not advocating anything fantastic, nor any striving after original effects or exaggerations." But she was relieved at the appearance of Alexandria Court, built in 1914 by the Heineman brothers in the style of "Italian villas, as we might call them," and "plastered with cement stucco, known as 'Gunite.'" Soon courts appeared in styles to suit every taste and

Gibson Court, built in 1914 at 1060 N. Normandie, Hollywood, designed by Frank M. Tyler

budget—Mission Revival, Spanish Colonial Revival, Mediterranean, English Country Tudor, Italianate, American Colonial, and even modernist. They were often paired with the Southern California ideal: exotic landscaping, maintained by gardeners so renters could relax and enjoy their little portion of the dream.

Bowen Court still exists, though it is now fenced off from the street and gated. Its palms, camphor trees, and jade now tower over and almost engulf the cottages. Cats are everywhere, as are crows and parrots, whose cawing almost drowns out sounds of the cars on the street. The sense of connection remains. Residents amble in a leisurely pace back and forth along the central path; a few sit on their porches watching life go by. Several of the tenants at Bowen Court were lifers.

Sharon Chivers, a twenty-five-year veteran, raised her two daughters there. They could run up and down in the wide pathway, safe from cars, and meet all the neighbors. "They had so many honorary aunts and uncles and grandparents. It was their place to play in a way that a lot of kids weren't able to." Her children have moved on, but she perambulates through the court with her friend Nancy Nagel. The entire effect is of a secret garden, bursting with fertility. It is utterly charming and picturesque, if not quite in the way its creators intended. Nagel recalls walking along its wooded pathway one time, feeling as if she was in *Sleeping Beauty* or *Cinderella*. "I thought, can I get the squirrels to clean my house like in the Disney movies? I like fairytale cottages, and that's what it feels like to me."

Downtown Los Angeles was packed with tall office and apartment buildings by 1913.

## The Bryson Apartment-Hotel: Living the High Life

Shortly after Bowen Court was built, an ambitious developer named Hugh W. Bryson welcomed tenants to his grand undertaking: the Bryson Apartment-Hotel on Wilshire Boulevard at Rampart Avenue. While the bungalow court was taking over the landscape, a different alternative to the single-family house was being imported from New York and Chicago: the multistory apartment complexes known as apartment-hotels, complete with doormen and housekeeping, and bookable for short and long stays. In the 1910s, they started to spread west from downtown along Wilshire Boulevard and into Hollywood. The grandest early example was the Bryson. This ten-story, U-shaped pile was made of white stucco concrete with a profusion of Beaux Arts and Mediterranean Revival styling, and marble entry stairs guarded by stone lions. It was built in a mere six months to a design by the architects F. Noonan and C.H. Kysor. Six hundred grandees attended the opening party on Valentine's Day in 1913, reported the *Los Angeles Times*, which excitedly described touring the ballroom on the tenth floor as well as the library, billiards room, and dressing and smoking rooms, all decked out with "magnificent rugs, fine paintings, and rare plants … in the pergolas." Its three hundred rooms and ninety-six serviced apartments featured mahogany woodwork and new inventions like hideaway wall beds in the living rooms that doubled as bedrooms, an all-in-one living space that would nowadays be described as a bachelor apartment or studio. The Bryson was fully occupied within two days, according to the *Los Angeles Times*, which gushed that it was "the finest of its kind in the country, not even excepting the famous structures of similar character on Riverside Drive in New York." Like today's studios, the Bryson and the

**Postcard of the Bryson Apartment-Hotel, date unknown**

apartment buildings that followed it attracted the young couples and many singles who were trying their luck in Los Angeles. Ballrooms and other social spaces were common in such buildings. The typology was adapted to embrace the Southern California lifestyle: it had its own parking garage, and a stately garden sat out front. In a deal to build higher than was permissible back then, on a site that previously held two single-family homes, the structure was set back a hundred feet and installed tennis courts, a wide lawn with stone urns, and ornamental shrubs and palm trees. The Bryson's landscaping, wrote the *Los Angeles Times* in the year it opened, "constitutes one of its principal charms."

Those features have been removed, and the once

grand Bryson Apartment-Hotel is now the Bryson Family Apartments, managed by EAH Housing, a nonprofit housing corporation. The building was spared from demolition after descending downmarket in the 1940s and spending several decades as a movie location, playing the role of dilapidated mansion, most famously in the 1947 adaptation of Raymond Chandler's novel *The Lady in the Lake*. In 1999, it was adaptively remodeled by the Los Angeles Housing Partnership into housing for people earning below the poverty line. The glitz has gone from both the building and its surroundings, as the neighborhood fell out of fashion. But it is still guarded by stone lions and shields marked with "The Bryson," and its lacey carved stonework is visible on the façade. While the ballroom, billiards tables, and library have disappeared, there is a vestige of the building's social dimension: the lowest floor became home to the nonprofit arts organization Heart of Los Angeles (HOLA). But the Bryson set the tone for a type of home that would proliferate in Los Angeles despite efforts to keep the region filled with low-rise houses— the serviced apartment tower with lavish shared amenities and open-air spaces, ideal for the temporary resident wanting an immediate sense of welcome and a connection to the California outdoors.

The bungalow court was later rendered defunct by rising costs of land and onerous parking mandates. In the early days, builders chose how much parking to fit on the site. Mark Vallianatos, executive officer for innovation at L.A. Metro, who has researched zoning's impact on housing in Los Angeles, explains that in 1931, the city of L.A. became one of the first places in the world to require parking spaces for new homes: specifically, "garage space on the premises for at least one automobile" for each unit in new multifamily buildings with twenty or more apartments. Then, in 1934, the city expanded this rule to cover all new

multifamily housing, from duplexes on up. This mandatory parking, combined with yard requirements introduced the same year, took so much space that there was no longer enough room on most properties for the housing and a central court. Henceforward, the provision of parking spaces would be a primary driver in the form and appearance of housing in Los Angeles, but it did not kill the court as an organizing principle of L.A. multifamily housing. As for the apartment-hotel, it initially seemed to be only a bit player in L.A.'s housing story. But together the bungalow court and apartment hotel laid the foundation for a succession of multifamily housing types in Los Angeles that have common ground at their core: courtyard housing and its descendants; garden apartments; mid- and high-rise loft, co-living, and condo-hotel buildings; contemporary low-income housing centered on shared space; and the low-rise compound with newly added ADUs.

In quite different ways, both of those precedents delivered some of the privacy of a single-family home along with access to outdoor space. Both offered residents a sense of a self-contained community. The bungalow court and apartment-hotel emerged as Los Angeles was developing—first via train lines and then the car—in thinly dispersed housing on long linear strips and in subdivisions that lacked the density and the vibrant commercial and public gathering spaces of older cities. Thousands of people had left family and friends to chase their dreams in L.A. Many came alone. The sprawl and the car and the isolation of houses must have compounded the feeling of anonymity. The new arrivals taking up residence in pastoral Pasadena or on the outer edges of Wilshire Boulevard might feel rootless in the vast, undifferentiated Los Angeles basin. So a community could be found at home, in the courtyard of a bungalow complex or in the lobby or ballroom of an apartment-hotel.

# 02

# COURTYARD HOUSING
## Marketing a Fantasy

If the bungalow court was a hit in the early 1910s, it boomed in the 1920s, so much so that the *Los Angeles Times*, in 1924, published a letter to the editor in the form of a poem called "Life in a Bungalow Court":

> Did you ever live in a bungalow court, and
>     have neighbors a plenty, of every sort?
> With each little cot filled to its doors, so that
>     some of them surely must sleep on the
>     floors.
> Some from the north and some from the south.
>     Such a lot all so different and yet so alike,
>     doing their best their landlord to fight …
> Some find life easy in this land of the sun and
>     take things as they find them, and have lots
>     of fun.
> There is a phonograph playing in each little cot,
>     and on Sunday mornings of noise there's a
>     lot.
> The motors buzz in and the motors buzz out.
>     Everyone going a different route.

*Opposite: Villa d'Este, 1928*

The courts morphed into every conceivable formation and architectural style. It might be square or rectangular or narrowed to a wide pathway or rounded into an oval. Complexes sat on flat land or sometimes scaled steep hills, as in Echo Park. The one- or two-story building around the court would sometimes enclose one or two sides, in an L or a T. It could be a three-sided U-shape or a full square. It was open to the street, or it was gated. Parking was added, first discreetly at the rear, then at the side, the front, and underneath. The detached cottages, or bungalows, became uneconomic for builders as the cost of land rose, so they morphed into solid wings of apartments; extra stories were added, becoming "courtyard housing," sometimes in deluxe Spanish styling and with the court now known as a "patio." Two enterprising duos put the patio on the map: the architects F. Pierpont and Walter S. Davis, and the self-taught designer-developers Arthur and Nina Zwebell. But they both got their start with fanciful developments in what became known as the Storybook style: French Norman meets English Tudor, at a scale a hobbit would feel at home in.

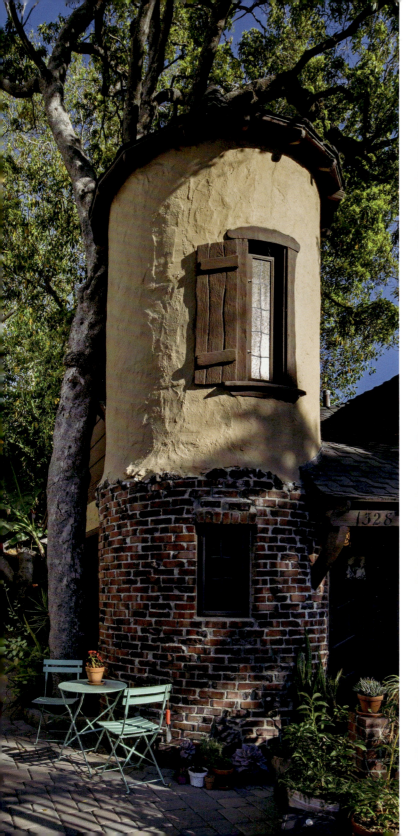

## Storybook Villages: A Real-Life Fairytale

F. Pierpont and Walter S. Davis were two of five children of a Baltimore architect named Henry Davis. Pierpont traveled extensively in France, Italy, and Southern Spain. Henry Davis visited Europe in uniform, serving in World War I. In 1919, the brothers set up shop in Los Angeles. Their first big project, French Village, was built in 1920 on a V of land where Highland and Cahuenga meet, at the mouth of the Cahuenga Pass (it was later demolished to make way for the Hollywood Freeway). Five houses boasting half-timbering, cone-topped towers and turrets, steep, tiled roofs, and gabled dormers, surrounded a picturesque garden with a curving bridge and sycamore trees. Perhaps Walter S. was inspired by actual places he had seen during wartime. Perhaps French Village was a valentine to an idealized France before the hell of the Great War. It was certainly catnip to Hollywood actors and craftspeople who lived happily at French Village through the 1940s; its residents are said to have included actor Wallace Beery and the costume designers Adrian and Irene Lentz. And French Village likely caught the eye of Arthur and Nina Zwebell, a highly creative pair who arrived in Los Angeles in the early 1920s, joining the waves of immigrants coming to try their luck in that decade.

The Zwebells were both raised in the Midwest. Nina was a trained musician with a gift for interior design. Arthur was a self-taught inventor and car nut who created a variant of the tire vulcanizer, a machine to mold traction patterns onto a tire, as well as a sporty two-seater that could be attached to the chassis of a regular Ford. They married in 1914 and set up businesses in Milwaukee, Wisconsin—Nina as an interior decorator, Arthur running a car dealership with his brothers. Then, armed with around $35,000 in savings,

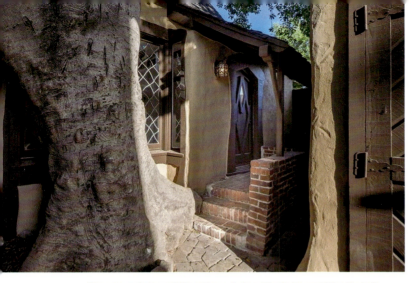

Opposite and above: **Village Court, designed by Arthur and Nina Zwebell.**

the Zwebells moved to Los Angeles and set themselves up as designer-builders for a community already steeped in make-believe: Hollywood. Their first project was a bungalow court aptly named Quaint Village, at the southeast corner of Ridgewood and Fernwood Avenues in Hollywood. It was every bit as faux-quaint as the Davis brothers' French Village. The Zwebells lived and worked at Quaint Village while they built two other courts that same year, 1923: Village Court, and Mexican Village, known now as Villa Primavera.

Village Court, at 1328 North Formosa Avenue in Hollywood, is one of the most notable extant examples of a bungalow court in the Storybook style. It has been called variously the Hansel and Gretel Cottages and Chaplin Court, due to a rumor that the complex was commissioned by silent movie star and director Charlie Chaplin. However, an application for Los Angeles Historic-Cultural Monument status states that the Zwebells' client was in fact a real estate investor named Louis Casler, and the original name of the place was Casler Village Court.

The "village" consisted of four half-timbered cottages with charmingly wonky plastered walls, wooden shutters, and brick steps arranged along a winding, stone-paved court on which sit soft-green metal cafe chairs and tables. The cottages are tiny; the smallest is 560 square feet and the largest is 700 square feet. But that did not deter Hollywood royalty from living there over the years and making merry under the trees in the shared court, or at least that is the story. Chaplin himself is said to have lived there for a while, as well as John Barrymore, Rudolph Valentino, Douglas Fairbanks (Sr.), Errol Flynn, Judy Garland, Marilyn Monroe, and, more recently, the actor Patrick Dempsey.

## Andalusia: Nostalgic Romanticism

Villages fit for Middle Earth had their charms, but it turned out that the denizens of Hollywood in the 1920s preferred a Spanish-style backdrop to their lives. This suited both the Davises and the Zwebells just fine. Both duos were passionate about dwellings arranged around a court or, specifically, the Mediterranean "patio." Just how they developed these for Los Angeles was later unpacked by three aficionados of the style—James Tice, Stefanos Polyzoides, and Roger Sherwood—in their brilliant 1982 book *Courtyard Housing in Los Angeles: A Typological Analysis.* The patio, or hardscaped courtyard, which often featured channels of water and shade trees, was well-known to Southern California architects partly due to the presence of the missions, and partly due to a fascinating quirk of history, per the authors. American architects of means would traditionally travel to Europe to study the gothic and neoclassical palaces and churches of France and Italy. During World War I, however, these countries were off limits. So architects went instead to the Iberian Peninsula in Southern Spain. They fell in love with Andalusia in Moorish Spain, similar to Southern California in its climate, landscape, and crystalline light, and home to the remarkable Alhambra in Granada and the courtyard houses of Seville. They admired the *casas de vecinos* (apartment

El Cabrillo, designed by Arthur and Nina Zwebell, offers a theatrical sense of arrival into the hidden court.

houses), *alcazars* (urban palaces), *haciendas* (freestanding farms), and *callejons* (dead-end urban streets). The courtyard buildings were rooted in Islamic architecture, which favored enclosed, or "paradise" gardens secluded from the outside. According to the architectural historian Banister Fletcher, a building in this tradition "tended to contain its garden rather than be contained within it, reflecting the concept of the garden as a space made by man." It was the inverse of a rustic, detached bungalow sitting in a grassy lawn. And it was adapted to Southern California's open lifestyle, absent the ancient social strictures.

Armed with this inspiration and the construction skills of set builders in Hollywood, the Zwebells, Davises, and others began creating gorgeous courtyard housing, some of it still standing in residential neighborhoods including West Hollywood, Hollywood, Los Feliz, Echo Park, and Pasadena. Typically the structures are soft white or cream or pale orange with red-tiled roofs and decorative tile and balustrades, overhangs, gates, light fixtures in ornamental wood and metalwork. The entrances are often discreet—a small gate or a narrow, dark corridor that opens dramatically onto a light, bright inner courtyard paved with brick or stone, with tiled fountains, channels of cooling water, and often lush, tropical planting. Apartments face the court, and often open onto wooden walkways on the second story, which is accessible through an outside staircase from the court. These are hidden paradises, presenting a fairly mute façade to the street. Perhaps this appealed to the many actors who lived in these idylls. Young Hollywood could behave badly inside these walls, out of sight of passersby. Or maybe this inner court, with its Romeo-and-Juliet balconies, appealed to thespians because it was simply the perfect stage for the daily drama of life.

Even though they had no formal training in

A trickling fountain and lush planting create a secluded paradise at El Cabrillo.

architecture, the Zwebells had a good understanding of its history and called themselves "ancients" because of their preference for historic styles. In 1923, they embarked on the design and construction of six stunning courts inspired by Andalusia. One of them was even called the Andalusia. Villa Primavera, originally called Mexican Village, was their first, built at 1300 North Harper Avenue in West Hollywood. It featured ten units on two stories around a court with a tiled fountain, lush blooms, and a looming outdoor fireplace with a stone relief of the Madonna and Child. Balconies in carved, roughened wood complete the effect. "It is one of the great, early L.A. courtyard apartment buildings," says architect Ian McIlvaine, who has lived in two period L.A. courtyard buildings from the early 1920s. "Courtyards are no guarantee that residents will commune—there are modern apartment buildings with courtyards that are merely leftover space—but these classic L.A. courtyard apartment buildings are very inviting." In recent years, Villa Primavera has become

El Cabrillo, interior with decorative tile, railings, and engraved stone fireplace

melancholy, perhaps because most of the residents have left in a process of attrition and the building has become dilapidated as new owners have prepared for an overhaul of the century-old plumbing and other repairs. One resident who has lived there since 1998 expressed sadness at the departure of her neighbors, saying, "I love the building because it stood for, fostered, and created a community." The director Nicolas Ray lived there at one point and was so taken with the evocative backdrop, he recreated it in noirish black and white in his 1950 noir film *In a Lonely Place*. The failing screenwriter Dix Steele (Humphrey Bogart) and the would-be actress Laurel Gray (Gloria Grahame) glimpse each other across the courtyard and a tragic passion ensues.

The Zwebells' next courts were ever more elaborate. The Andalusia, built in 1926, had three separate but linked courts, the first of which, appropriately for L.A., was for cars. El Cabrillo (1928), at the southeast corner of Franklin and Grace Avenues in Hollywood, went a step further. Unlike their earlier

projects, which were constructed, backdrop-style, out of wood frame and plaster, this two-story, ten-unit building was made out of masonry (concrete, brick-like blocks) and offered residents private balconies as well as the common patio. Its detailing—brick pavers, high-ceilinged interiors with exposed timber beams, a quatrefoil-shaped fountain, and second-floor walkways with decorative wood balustrades—projected the feeling of permanence of its architectural antecedents. It was commissioned by the movie mogul Cecil B. DeMille for—it is speculated—young actors coming out to Los Angeles, or for his daughter, Frances. Either way, it was one of L.A.'s most fashionable addresses and home to luminaries including Ann Harding, Lowell Sherman, and, in the 1960s, Divine. Then it took a dive. By the 1990s, the neighborhood was so distressed that remaining residents would "have to lie on the floor to avoid being hit by bullets flying through their windows," according to *Lost Hollywood* writer David Wallace. But El Cabrillo bounced back, having been

F.B. Lewis Courts, also known as Bella Vista Terrace, 1910

restored to perfection and turned into condominiums in 2009 by the developer Xorin Balbes.

The Davis brothers created two spectacular complexes: Roman Gardens in 1926 and the Villa d'Este in 1928. To the Spanish influences they added flavors of Italy, which Walter S. Davis had documented in dreamy watercolor paintings made during past travels. The Villa d'Este, named in homage to the splendid sixteenth-century villa in Tivoli, features a façade with the quoins and the high, square windows of Renaissance design, along with Corinthian-style pilasters on the exterior of the parking garage. Its pièce de résistance, however, is its inner court, which is visible only on passing through a dimly lit, deep terracotta corridor. At the end, visitors are greeted by whoosh of sunlight and a burst of lush planting, dominated, wrote the authors of *Courtyard Housing*, "by a fountain, from which water flows from the mouth of a lion mounted on a column, a copy from the Palazzo Bevilacqua in Bologna, Italy."

The drama of the hidden patio was the realization of an effect described in a 1915 book of stock plans entitled *California Garden City Homes* that was co-authored by Walter S. Davis. In making the case for courtyard housing in the Southland, he and his fellow writers described the houses of ancient Pompeii. From the streets, passersby would see only "walls unbroken by any opening except the doors. Entering the dark shadow doorway and pushing aside the heavy curtains one stepped out into a court, beautiful and brilliant." This arrangement lent itself to a more secluded kind of courtyard living than the Southern California bungalow court, whose semi-private shared area was exposed to the street even if it clearly was not intended for public use. The inner court added a sense of mystery and secrecy to the idea of home.

The era of dreamy Spanish-style courts proved to be short-lived, however, because the Depression put a stop to the runaway construction of the roaring twenties, and then parking mandates put the nail in

This wing of Bella Vista Terrace has some vestige of the building's original charm (2021)

the coffin. But courtyard living went on to take other forms. As for the indefatigable Zwebells, they quickly pivoted—to production design for the movies. Nina Zwebell went on to work as an interior and furniture designer. Arthur left the dream of Andalusia behind and in the mid-1930s even tried, without success, to launch a modular housing system. Ironically, this connected him to a group of designers that had no time for nostalgic architecture: the fledgling modernists, starting with Irving Gill.

## The Early Modernist Court: Health in Housing

If the Zwebells, the Davises, and other designer-builders were borrowing indiscriminately from the palaces and patios of old Europe, another band of designers was trying to slough off the legacy of tired aristocracies— while also experimenting with courtyard living. Most early courts in Southern California were slathered in

period revival styling, but there was a countertrend: a radically stripped-down look devoid of storybook romance. The styles, Chase says, "referenced different aspects of the California dream to lure people west—a nostalgic romanticism for one and utopian healthy living for the other." It was first introduced by the architect Irving Gill as far back as 1910, in the F.B. Lewis Courts, also known as Bella Vista Terrace, in Sierra Madre, a few miles east of Pasadena. Gill, known then as the architect of fine houses in San Diego, wanted to design homes for low-income workers, a group he felt was typically "ignored by architecture" according to Esther McCoy in *Five California Architects*. So he and Lewis built a complex of eight cottages on a square site, each with its own garden that led into a central community garden with a large pergola in the center. The structures were soft-white, cube-like forms with simple round-arched openings. The outer, or rear, walls of each cottage were connected, creating a continuous wall that was flush with the street, Mexican-style, not detached as with the craftsman-style courts. Gill, who had himself traveled west to improve his health, was on a mission to create sanitary dwellings filled with natural light, labor-saving devices, and smooth surfaces where no dust or vermin could gather. He aspired to this early minimalism for reasons of both health and beauty. Writing for *The Craftsman* in May 1916, he extolled "the simple cube house with creamy walls, sheer and plain, rising boldly into the sky, unrelieved by cornices or overhang of roof." This aesthetic contains echoes of the local Mission tradition, but it also bore the stirrings of European modernism. The architecture critic Esther McCoy was a fan of Bella Vista Terrace, writing in her 1960 book *Five California Architects*, "There was a reference for the individual and the plan that has never been equaled in the field of minimum housing." Only one third of the site was built on, leaving the rest for personal and shared outdoor space. Unfortunately, Bella Vista Terrace fell victim to its own success, in terms of its social goals. The dwellings were so appealing that the owner decided to charge far more than a regular worker could afford. More recently, poor Bella Vista Terrace became a bowdlerized version of itself as later owners built a ranch house and a backyard pool in the onetime shared court, obliterating the design's communal heart.

In 1919, Gill designed another variant on a bungalow court, which stands in pristine condition near the beach in Santa Monica: Horatio West Court. This complex of four small white concrete houses is bisected by a cruciform pathway. Its beauty lies in the combination of simplicity and complexity. The dwellings have similar plans but vary in their window arrangements and orientation to take advantage of the sun and views. Interlocking rooms give the massing of each dwelling a cubist feel. The bare white walls are offset by green-painted window frames; those windows, a specialty of Gill's, come in a multitude of forms and exposures—clerestories, skylights, and corner openings—that give each home a lantern-like quality when it is lit up at night. For residents, the daily passage of sunlight through the houses is key to the livability of these relatively petite spaces.

Santa Monica preservationist Margaret Bach and the architect Glen Small led a group that saved Horatio West Court in the 1970s. By that time, Gill's mini-masterpiece had fallen into decrepitude, occupied by drug addicts and visiting rats. The investors bought Horatio West Court in 1973 and painstakingly restored it, converting it into four condominiums. Each lived there for several years. There were challenges, says Bach: the concrete walls were cold, and there was no room for expansion with a growing family. But, Bach adds, their home was exquisite in many ways. She recalls the high clerestory windows in the small kitchens. "They were perfectly positioned for cross-ventilation … there was a beautiful little staircase at the heart of each unit that wound its way up like a conch shell, accented at midpoint by a little triangular ledge with a window, bringing light into the stairwell. Every design move, from the height of the ceilings, to the dimensions of each room, to the position of the windows, was brilliant and considered." Vitally, each dwelling has its own walled outdoor space, offering residents privacy, while a shared seating area in the graveled central court provides opportunities for gathering with neighbors. The configuration works perfectly for both daily living and social occasions, says longtime resident Barbara Whitney. "Living here has given me a huge appreciation for communal living," she says. "This was the embodiment of 'it takes a village.' My daughter, Kate, who went on to study architecture and historic preservation in college, grew up playing in the gated safety of the courtyard with other children—and developed her photography skills capturing Gill's light and volumes."

## Preserving the Fantasy

Bungalow courts and courtyard housing are so delightful—even those that were not especially grand in their day—that of all the multifamily housing types in Los Angeles they have been seen as aspirational, not declassé, and have taken hold in the imagination as a vernacular style of Los Angeles. After all, these once-themed environments now have the added appeal of being genuinely old. Thousands have gone, of course, as the giant maw of Los Angeles real estate development gobbles them up, but some are being saved, an effort that got underway in the late 1990s when preservationists managed to get St. Andrews Bungalow Court—fifteen Colonial Revival bungalows constructed around a central court by an anonymous builder in 1919-1920—listed on the National Register of Historic Places. "St. Andrews Bungalow Court is an excellent representation of an important and once common, but increasingly rare, building type in Los Angeles," wrote the applicants. The nonprofit Hollywood Community Housing Corporation bought the dilapidated building and transformed it into subsidized housing for people with HIV/AIDS. It then served as the home for the adorably hapless Dave Seville (played by Jason Lee) in the blockbuster *Alvin and The Chipmunks*, fixing in the minds of a new generation the charms of courtyard living in Los Angeles. Or they are being incorporated into larger developments, as happened to the Ramona, a 1923 courtyard apartments project formed by three two-story buildings configured in a U-shape in West Hollywood, with a row of trees between the buildings and a large fountain out front. The Ramona was built at the same time as Arthur and Nina Zwebell's Villa Primavera just up the street, and the name came from an oil-painted sign hung in the front courtyard, bearing the name of Helen Hunt Jackson's famed book

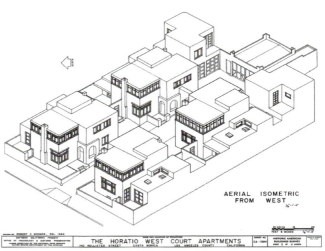

**Above: Horatio West Court and its aerial axiomatic.**

sentimentalizing Mexican colonial life. The building was bought in the aughts by new owners who wanted to knock it down and replace it with market-rate condos. The residents, a tight-knit group as one finds in so many courts, fought back. The *Los Angeles Times* weighed in, and the city came up with a win-win: the developers got permission to build a five-story condominium building in an L-shape around one end of the site, between the back of one flank of the Ramona and the new structure. In return for an extra story, known as a height bonus, they agreed to maintain the Ramona, almost intact, as low-income dwellings. Ric Abramson, now the City Architect for West Hollywood, led the restoration of the Ramona and designed the 2010 condo structure, named Harper West Hollywood, in a way that models the best of multifamily design today—with private and shared spaces, plenty of light, and a range of different apartment sizes. "I was challenged," he says, "with creating a building that automatically would have been completely out of scale, because of that transfer of the density." So he broke down the scale of the new building with a strategic and lively layering of balconies, terraces, decks, stoops, exterior stairs, and a pathway, which is effectively a new court between the old and the new structures. The result is affordable and market-rate multifamily dwellings, all on the same site, extending the court tradition into the future.

Some old courts are being salvaged and transformed into studios for people on the move—like 227 Beach Street in Ocean Park, Santa Monica. Built in 1924 and now meticulously remodeled by Isabelle Duvivier, the court is complete with a contemporary landscape of olive trees and native plantings. On completion in 2022, Duvivier anticipated young professionals would lease its 400-square-foot units with market-rate rents. Her own experience of courtyard living was cross-generational.

She grew up in a two-story apartment building centered on a tree-filled court a few blocks north of this bungalow court. "My first boyfriend lived upstairs and my sister's best friend lived across the courtyard. And that was our little world. We played with all the kids that lived in that building, and it was great."

Now, as then, these contrived environments are a stage set to live in, and at their most luxe they were very well-suited, writes Laura Chase, "to the needs of a transient population drawn to Hollywood in part by the chance to live in an exotic, garden-like setting while pursuing stardom." They also had a reverse impact, influencing scenography while scenography impacted residential design. Court historians have theorized that Walt Disney based the background of his groundbreaking animated movie *Snow White and the Seven Dwarfs*, released in 1937, on a three-quarter-scale Bavarian village court, constructed in 1928, that he could see from his workplace at the first Walt Disney Studios, then located in Silver Lake. The Spanish-style courts have routinely served as sets or inspirations for shows whose drama takes place within a tight community—most famously *Melrose Place*, whose fictional 4646 Melrose Place courtyard was partly filmed at the El Pueblo Apartments at 4616 Greenwood Place in Los Feliz. Darren Star, the producer of the hit show, based the steamy drama on his own experience living in a courtyard building as a young writer-waiter in L.A. "Most of the inhabitants were in their twenties," he later told the *New York Times*. "Everybody had roommates. There was a lot of sex." His building was not a gracious Mediterranean fantasy, however. "It was one of those '60s-era Motel 6-looking places. Really ugly."

Opposite: Fans of *Melrose Place* still make pilgrimages to El Pueblo Apartments.

# 03

# EUROPEAN MODERNISM COMES TO L.A.

rving Gill's stripped-down bungalow courts of the 1910s seemed to have grown from the sandy soil of the Southland. But he was in fact a prescient player in the larger story of architecture that was unfolding on the international stage. Gill was born in 1870, the same year as a Viennese architect who was having a profound influence in Europe: Adolf Loos. Loos came to the U.S. in 1893 and studied the towers in Chicago designed by Louis Sullivan and his partner, Dankmar Adler, at almost exactly the same time Gill was working at that office. Loos was amazed by the bracing functionalism and modernity of Chicago's new skyscrapers, as well as the efficient mechanical tools Americans used in construction. He returned to Vienna as a proselytizer for the machine aesthetic—smooth, unadorned buildings that looked industrially made— and gave a talk in 1910 called Ornament and Crime, later published as a book that became an essential text for architecture students. In essence, he argued, florid decoration on buildings of the period was a

sign of moral degeneracy. "The evolution of culture is synonymous with the removal of ornament from utilitarian objects," he announced.

His ideas were taken up by the Swiss-French architect Le Corbusier and the German Walter Gropius, who founded the Bauhaus school in 1919 in Dessau. These men would have an enormous impact on the direction of architecture in the twentieth century. They rejected the weighty, ornamented masonry buildings of the past with classical columns and symmetrical layouts and instead envisioned structures made of new, factory-made materials such as concrete and steel, arranged in interlocking planes with glass, abstract in shape and asymmetrical in plan. Cubist painters were an inspiration. So was the modernity of America—its cars, streamlined factories, and jazz music, as well as the skyscrapers soaring in Chicago and New York. European modernists were impressed by Frank Lloyd Wright, with his innovative Prairie houses in the Midwest that were long and low with an open floor plan and broad, overhanging eaves. Both Wright and the European avant-garde deeply admired Japanese art and architecture: the flattened space of the prints, and

**Opposite: Manola Court, designed by R.M. Schindler**

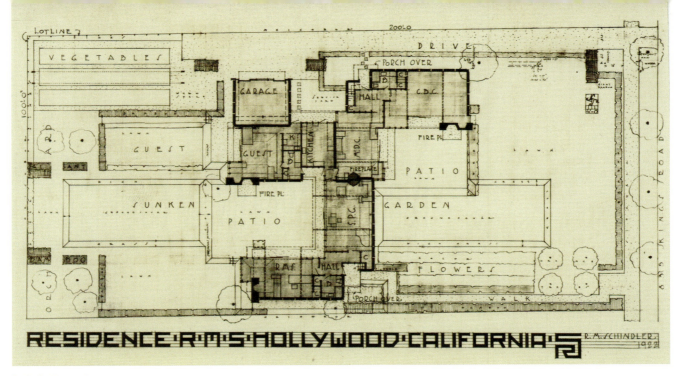

**Schindler House plan**

the simplicity, economy, and flexibility of living spaces, achieved with sliding doors and translucent shoji screen partitions. This was not simply a stylistic movement, however; the early modernists bound their aesthetic impulses to a social mission, in response to the war that left millions homeless and an industrial age that had created energetic cities that were also petri dishes for ill health and deep poverty. They believed it was the responsibility of architects (who traditionally designed civic buildings and private houses for the rich) to house the masses in healthful homes filled with natural light and air. While his counterparts were preaching this philosophy in the intellectual capitals of Europe, Gill was quietly practicing it, far away on the western edge of the U.S.; and to it he was adding something softer, the warm, simple white massing and courtyard planning of Southern California, with clambering vines and abundant vegetation. He died in 1936 in relative obscurity, but his legacy lived on, in highly original dwellings by later architects in Los Angeles who

synthesized the innovations in Europe with those under their noses in California.

## R.M. Schindler

First came Rudolph, or R.M., Schindler, an expat from Vienna who had imbibed the ideas of Adolf Loos and traveled to the U.S. in 1914 to work for a Chicago firm before being hired—for almost no pay—by his hero, Frank Lloyd Wright. Wright sent him to Los Angeles to work on the Hollyhock House for Aline Barnsdall, which started construction in 1919 while Wright was working on the Tokyo Imperial Hotel in Japan. In 1922, Schindler built his own extraordinary house on Kings Road in West Hollywood.

### SCHINDLER HOUSE

Schindler House on North Kings Road, now a nonprofit cultural venue also known as the MAK Center, was essentially a form of courtyard housing,

**Schindler House, rear court**

albeit for only two families—Rudolph and his wife Pauline, and his engineer-builder Clyde Chace and his wife Marian. It was shockingly new, made of tilt-up concrete panels, with slender vertical windows and sliding screens giving onto an inner grassy court at the back and front of the site. Chace had worked with Irving Gill on Horatio West Court and took from that experience both building tips and the tools to aid in the construction of Schindler's groundbreaking concrete structure, which, unlike Horatio West, was left exposed, with the raw concrete now an aesthetic effect. It also had a unique plan. Instead of two apartments with regular rooms, Schindler gave each occupant their own studio, intended to be multipurpose, and created open porches, or "sleeping baskets," on the roof. Schindler's studio was on the south side, and Pauline's was in the center. McCoy, who later worked for Schindler, described the building in her book *Five California Architects* as an S-shape, coiling "around the flat lot, gathering garden spaces within protecting

walls, and setting up barriers against the street. Exterior walls became interior walls for outdoor living rooms; the plan of the house divided the garden into three intimate areas." The fluid, undefined spaces, sliding screens, and framed views of the outside bring to mind Japanese domestic design. The rooms, which bled into the gardens, pioneered Southern California's "inside-outside" modern living, later spread worldwide through the poetic imagery of post-war, post-and-beam and glass Case Study Houses embedded in the landscape. The social arrangement took cues from Europe. Kathryn Smith, an architectural historian who wrote a book about the building, lived at Schindler House for five years with her mattress and her desk in one of the sleeping baskets. She points out that Schindler came from a continent where housing was expensive, land was in limited supply, and people routinely lived on top of each other. "So when he owned the lot on Kings Road, he didn't think about building the two-story house and studios only for himself and his wife. He

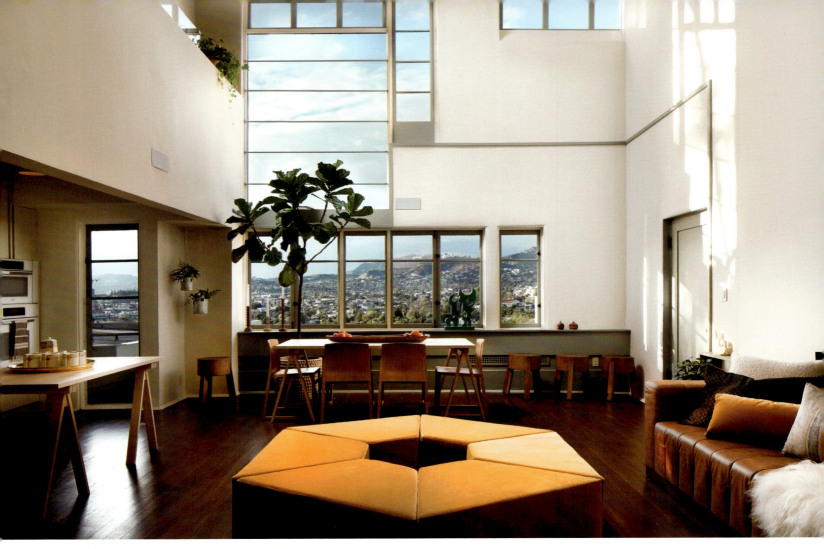

Manola Court studio, restored by Enclosures Architects

immediately thought of this communal aspect."

On completion of Schindler House in 1922, the house and its outdoor spaces became a hub of social gatherings and outré theater, dance, and music, driven in large part by the vital Pauline, whose parents had largely paid for the property. The Chaces left in the mid-1920s, and an old friend of Schindler, newly arrived in L.A., moved in: the architect Richard Neutra and his wife, Dione. The four lived together in this ultra-modern duplex for a few years, before a rift

grew between the two men and within the Schindler marriage. Later, the divorced Schindlers each resided in half the property. Following his death, Pauline lived on the north side and rented out the downstairs studios on the south, the upstairs sleeping basket, and a guest studio. She vetted renters, who were all architecture aficionados, and laid down the law. When Smith and her cohorts decided to reprise the social aspect of the place by installing a shared dining table in the court, they had to get permission from Pauline. Smith recalls her saying, "'I will approve of it but it has to have a design review.' So it had to be a certain kind of material, had to be a certain kind of shape, and have no ornamental aspects to it." Smith wound up buying a simple wood picnic table with benches, and afterward tenants ate together every day.

## MANOLA COURT

After building his eponymous house, Schindler plunged into designing and building a string of residential landmarks—including several remarkable apartment buildings. The first was the 1923 Pueblo Ribera Court in La Jolla, twelve units configured so the roof of one became the patio of another. In the late 1930s, he built the Mackey Apartments on South Cochran Avenue and two complexes in Silver Lake: Bubeshko (1939) and Falk (1940). A decade later, he built the now-landmarked 1949 Laurelwood Apartments in Studio City, which consists of twenty two-bedroom dwellings lining a staggered pathway. Each has a private patio and glass interior walls that transmit light and air throughout the units. To look at them is to be amazed by the intricate arrangement of angled walls and windows, each poised to take advantage of the sun. As for the arrangement of the dwellings along a shared pathway, it brings to mind the Spanish *callejon*, or dead-end urban street, much admired by the Spanish Colonial revivalists. Perhaps one of his most intriguing multifamily buildings, however, is a courtyard complex named Manola Court, aka the Sachs Apartments, in Silver Lake. Unlike Schindler's other designs, which were delivered as a complete concept, Manola evolved over many years between 1926 and 1939. It was commissioned by the ceramicist Herman Sachs, and has been undergoing a long and meticulous rehabilitation by current owner Paul Finegold with Enclosures Architects and Terremoto

landscape architects. The project started out as a little Spanish bungalow on Edgecliffe Drive, which Sachs asked Schindler to expand and modernize; they then spent thirteen years adding dwellings—sixteen in all, each with a private entrance and private terrace. The apartments cascade down a steep slope to Lucille Avenue, with a stepped central court in the heart of the building. Finegold and his design team have enhanced the central court, adding a rich mix of plantings along with benches to invite residents to hang out, which became a magnet during the pandemic lockdown. The apartments vary in size, from a jewel of a Douglas-fir-clad studio of 409 square feet in a one-time crawlspace, to a penthouse with a panoramic view of L.A. at the top; but all feature the dining nooks that became a Schindler trademark, along with his varied ceiling heights, multiple sources of natural and electric light, visible structure, and exposed materials. They also exude an intense warmth. Not for Schindler, cold modernism.

## Richard Neutra

While Schindler was crafting his groundbreaking, modernist take on the California court, so too was his sometime friend and professional rival Richard Neutra. Neutra had also left Vienna to work for Frank Lloyd Wright and arrived in Los Angeles in the early 1920s, evidently stirring up some local interest. The *Hollywood Daily Citizen* ran a small notice on April 11, 1925, about a talk to be given at the Hollywood Branch Library by a "European" named Richard Neutra, a "noted architect" of the "modern-Individualistic School," who was newly arrived in Southern California. The article went on to offer readers a helpful definition of the "individualist" in architecture: "One who follows none of the pre-established architectural styles, one who does not adopt Grecian, Roman, Gothic, 'Spanish,' or other already

Neutra configured Strathmore Apartments to follow the hillside topology and interweave indoor and outdoor space.

existing types to the requirements of his period. He is the creator of the [sic] different sort of a new style, of an individual type of architectural design."

Richard Neutra was a "European" par excellence. He was from a socially progressive family with connections to the leading cultural figures of the time. Neutra was a school friend of Sigmund Freud's son, Ernst, and his elder siblings played chamber music with Arnold Schoenberg, recounts Neutra's son, Raymond. Like Schindler, he was an admirer of Adolf Loos, the Viennese crusader against ornament in architecture. In the early 1920s he went to work in the Berlin office of the famed architect Erich Mendelsohn, helping him with the design of the remarkable expressionist Einstein Tower near Berlin (the *Hollywood Daily Citizen* credited Neutra alone for this building) as well as Zehlendorf, a cluster of four houses in suburban Berlin in a bold, stripped-down cubist style. While he was in Germany, the Bauhaus design school was active in Weimar, promising to tackle the problem of housing with a new "rationalist" approach to mass housing, using industrial materials and methods of fabrication. Meanwhile, the Austrian capital was in its socialist "Red Vienna" period. For sixteen years after the war and the collapse of the Hapsburg empire, the Austrian Social Democratic Workers' Party ran Vienna and undertook an ambitious public housing program, building four hundred public housing blocks to house 200,000 people, a tenth of the population. So when Neutra left for America in 1923, he was steeped in radical ideas about housing. He was also not yet softened by the California climate and spirit. As Esther McCoy pointed out, there was a big difference between Neutra and Schindler. Neutra arrived after World War I, while Schindler—deemed

**Resident Bill Bouchey talks with the author outside his Strathmore apartment.**

an enemy alien during wartime—had arrived in 1914, missing out on that cataclysm. He was able to bloom in easy, liberating California and escaped the stern influence of the rationalists in Neutra's orbit. Their work, noted Schindler, was "an expression of the minds of people who lived through the First World War, clad in uniforms, housed in dugouts, forced into utmost efficiency and meager sustenance, with no thought for joy, charm, warmth."

Nevertheless, in those early halcyon days Schindler and Neutra formed a team, creating a firm called the Architectural Group for Industry and Commerce (AGIC), and worked on a design for the League of Nations building in Geneva, a storied design competition which Le Corbusier won. Neutra also busied himself designing Rush City Reformed, a concept for a militantly rationalist mini-city which echoed Le Corbusier's Ville Radieuse, a utopian city of relentless tower blocks amidst vast open spaces, ringed by elevated highways. In ominous black charcoal, Neutra drew rows of concrete slabs for faceless workers along with homes, parks, and civic buildings. He divided the entire population into groups in his "uber scientific way," according to historian Kathryn Smith. Housing would be divided into separate sections, for single individuals, couples with no children, couples with children, and seniors. Meanwhile, he garnered a commission to design a real apartment building, Jardinette, which he realized with an assist from Schindler.

## JARDINETTE APARTMENTS

Jardinette Apartments, named after the French word for "little garden" (now named Marathon Apartments for the street on which it stands in East Hollywood), is a four-story, reinforced concrete structure in the shape of a shallow U, consisting of forty-three small studio and one-bedroom units with cantilevered balconies contained in three wings around an open landscaped courtyard. These balconies, shown in drawings with bountiful plants, were the "little gardens," and on completion the *Hollywood Examiner* described them as "gardens for cliff-dwellers!" The tiny apartments, ranging from 400 to 700 square feet, were organized quite efficiently according to a German modernist concept of *existenz minimum*, or minimum existence: open planning, built-in cabinets, fold-down Murphy beds, borrowed light via translucent glass panes in doors and partitions, and a kitchen planned as a "machine for the preparation of meals," so the cook could reach everything from one spot. This was the opposite of a spacious Los Angeles house. The small spaces were made to feel more roomy by horizontal ribbons of glass, and access, for some of the tenants, onto the balconies. While Neutra is generally credited with leading the Jardinette project, the interiors bear the stamp of Schindler, with ingenious built-ins, hidden sources of lighting, and warm wood finishes.

Jardinette was commissioned by a New York developer named Joseph H. Miller. He had stormed Los Angeles in the go-go 1920s with promises to erect a "veritable empire of luxurious Hollywood apartment houses," recounts Neutra historian Thomas S. Hines. He eschewed the "pre-established" architectural styles in vogue at the time, and promised ultra-modern buildings that would reflect the era's belief in the health-giving potential of fresh air and sunlight. Miller promised at least two panes of "violet-ray glass in the windows of each apartment." This newfangled (essentially single-pane) glass, was introduced in the late 1920s and touted as a transmitter of the beneficial ultraviolet rays of the sun—catnip for Neutra and many of his generation, who believed sunlight was bound up with health and could help cure tuberculosis and other ailments of

Ribbon windows flow into cantilevered balconies at the bracing Bauhaus-style Jardinette, also known as Marathon Apartments.

the industrial age. Miller also boasted an amenity in his apartment structures that became very popular in multifamily buildings in the 2020s—a runway for tenants' dogs—as well as one that did not: vaults for fur storage. As it turned out, though, Miller only built the smallest of his dream projects, the Jardinette Apartments. Then he went bankrupt and skipped town, eluding his creditors, including AGIC.

When Jardinette opened in 1929, it was radical: the first multifamily, international-style building to be built in America. But it did not receive the local fanfare—perhaps because its owner had disappeared—that accompanied the unveiling in the same year of a seminal residential building by Neutra: the Demonstration

Health House, a family home in the hills of Los Feliz for the naturopath Phillip Lovell. This house was "built for health," Lovell told readers in his "Care of the Body" column in the *Los Angeles Times*. The three-story, 4,000-square-foot steel frame and stucco building was anchored like a dry-docked ship to the hill, with free-flowing rooms that opened onto outdoor balconies, terraces, and sleeping porches. "It's a full, almost machine for healthy living," says Lyra Kilston, author of *Sun Seekers: The Cure of California*. "There were private areas where you could do your nude sunbathing, which was essentially akin to taking your vitamins every day." Around 15,000 people packed a three-day public viewing of the house in December 1929. Not everyone loved it, however. One visitor was overheard calling it "moon architecture," and even the clients, the Lovells, are said to have thought the house too clinical.

So too was Jardinette—even to its admirers. "Even to today's eye the Jardinette Apartments are startlingly severe with its lack of ornament, flat roof, and long planes alternating with banks of regular lines of steel-framed windows," wrote historical consultant Barbara Lamprecht in a 2017 application for a Mills Act tax exemption. In its time, perhaps it was an oddity, a luxury apartment building delivered in the ascetic style of social housing in Europe, offering garden living that was completely unlike the courtyard housing so popular at the time. But it was a hit with the avant-garde. A fulsome review appeared in the *Christian Science Monitor*—written by none other than Schindler's ex-wife, Pauline. The building was chosen along with three of Neutra's others for inclusion in the hugely influential 1932 MOMA exhibition, *The International Style*, curated by Henry-Russell Hitchcock and Philip Johnson. It was also the only one of two American apartment buildings out of fifty selected for inclusion in *The Modern Flat*, a book published in London in 1937 that showcased multifamily housing across Europe by the leaders of the modern movement, such as Le Corbusier, Walter Gropius, and Marcel Breuer. Of all the groundbreaking apartment buildings in that book, Jardinette was the earliest of them all.

Jardinette ceased to be "luxury," when the neighborhood went into economic decline. The building suffered, going from startling severity to depressing dilapidation, until it was emptied and shuttered in 2018. But Jardinette was added to the National Register of Historic Places in 1986, designated as a City of Los Angeles Historic-Cultural Monument in 1988, and its most recent owners are rehabilitating it. Meanwhile, the development has proven prescient.

The building offered sleek, modern studio living with the amenities of luxury apartments, something that has become the norm in new multifamily housing. Even its plan, the three wings around a courtyard, is an arrangement that appears in contemporary mid-rise buildings in Los Angeles.

## STRATHMORE APARTMENTS

After Jardinette, Neutra went on to build a shining model of multifamily living that was more suited to its terrain, a variant on the stepped bungalow court found in very hilly parts of L.A. The Strathmore Apartments was one of four developments designed by Neutra in Westwood Village, a planned community that was growing up around UCLA. They were built after Neutra had spent more than a decade soaking up the regional culture, and the design was a fusion of influences: L.A.'s beloved courts, the International Style, and, according to Hines, the "elegantly stacked megastructures of the Southwest Pueblo Indians." Strathmore is an eight-unit complex stepping in pairs up an extremely steep site. The central stairway serves as a spine for the complex, and pathways lead off of this spine to the dwellings themselves, which are angular buildings in bare white stucco with aluminum-painted silver window frames, flat overhangs, and horizontal bands of glass. The hillside was naked when it was first built, and the units were stridently spartan. Their beauty lay in the interplay of solid and void, but as the garden grew, their tidy lines became softened and enhanced by lush, unkempt foliage.

The Strathmore Apartments eventually became enveloped in such a dense jungle of ferns and trees that it is difficult to see them. This is because half the site at Strathmore is open space. In 1937, land was still abundant and relatively cheap. But this ratio of building

Strathmore Apartments, 1937

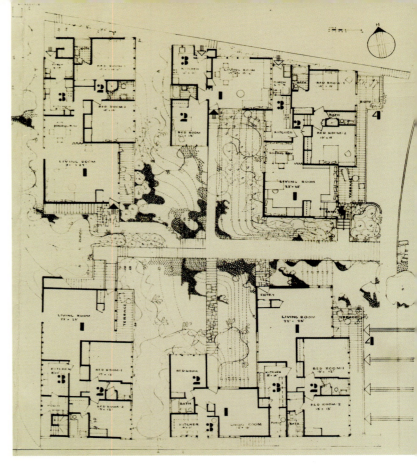

Strathmore Apartments plan

to land was also part of Neutra's design philosophy, which he termed biorealism. He embraced emerging theories about the mind/body/environment connection and believed buildings should create a union between man and nature. So a small apartment with a large amount of open space was better for one's well-being than living inside a larger home, hogging so much land that there was no outdoors. Inside the apartments, light and air comes from multiple sources: expansive windows facing south, clerestory windows on the north side, a corridor lit by a window on the west. Every unit is a little bit different; each one has views and direct access to the outdoors. Neutra's approach to apartment design was a reaction, says his son Raymond, to "his toddler dislike of the dark Victorian enclosed apartment

that he grew up in." It was perfect for sun-kissed Southern California.

It did not appear perfect right away, however. The very first residents at Strathmore were Neutra's family: Dione Neutra's sister, Regula, and their parents, Alfred and Lilly Niedermann, who had immigrated to Los Angeles. Hines writes that initially they were the only occupants, because prospective tenants found the buildings too "cold," "austere," and "industrial."

Before long, Strathmore attracted actors and artists drawn to its radical chic. The actress Luise Rainer moved in following a break-up from her husband, the playwright Clifford Odets. In a publicity coup for Neutra, he and Rainer were photographed together in her unit by Julius Shulman. He sat paternally in an

The actress Luise Rainer, posing with Richard Neutra

armchair, puffing on a pipe, while Rainer kneeled at his feet. In a letter to the architect, Rainer wrote that she had previously been afraid of modernism, but now loved its light and openness and "strange feeling of happiness and freedom." The designers Charles and Ray Eames lived there, and they posed in the apartment for a feature in *Mademoiselle* in which Ray declared, "We live in the most modern house in Los Angeles." For a time, Orson Welles lived at Strathmore, where he and actress Dolores del Rio are said to have carried on an affair.

The ability to conduct a discreet relationship attests to another dimension of the building that makes it work as a living space: its neighborliness, combined with the means to *avoid* the neighbors. The spine serves as an informal meeting spot for all the occupants, but Neutra purposely designed two routes to the dwellings at Strathmore Apartments. This way residents could use the central stairway or creep unnoticed up the back path, intended for deliveries. "One thing about my dad's work," says Raymond Neutra, "is that he was always

concerned with grouping people together, but giving them privacy." Since the 1970s, architecture writer Michael Webb has occupied a unit once lived in by Luise Rainer, and he remarks on that balance of private and semi-public: "I'm in a capsule that is part of a larger configuration that mediates between public and private. [The courtyard stair] is used by all my neighbors, so there's a constant vibe of people going up and down the stairs." The design was brilliant, says Lamprecht. "It was not quite single-family, not quite an apartment building, and laid out on a difficult site;" in sum, a perfect precedent for today's low-rise multifamily compounds.

Neutra built more apartment buildings in Westwood: Landfair, also in 1937, then the Kelton Apartments (1941), which the family owned, and Elkay Apartments (1948). Other progressive architects also built modern apartments nearby. One of them, built a decade later, was unmissable and a remarkable testament to the future: John Lautner's Sheats Apartments, an outlandish variant on stepped courtyard living.

04

# POST-WAR HOUSING
## Embracing the Future

When World War II ended, discharged veterans and former war workers flooded back into Los Angeles. There was so little housing available that thousands of vets were put in Quonset huts in Griffith Park. But there was also a spirit of optimism in the air as the baby boom began, the space age took off, and the innovation that had been applied to the war machine now went into the making of innovative homes, both single and multifamily. Apartments, says Chris Nichols, a longtime preservationist and senior editor at *Los Angeles* magazine, took cues from the improvements in mass housing. They were filled "with the same built-in conveniences, had the same walls of glass, integrated landscapes and gardens, new materials like Formica, even technologies like radiant heat and intercom systems." But they also built on the planning models of the prewar years, offering up courtyard housing for the technological age.

**Opposite: Sheats Apartments in 2019, designed by John Lautner**

## John Lautner: Sheats Apartments

In 1963, John Lautner, famed designer of space-age residential marvels in Los Angeles and Palm Springs, built the Sheats (now Sheats-Goldstein) residence, a stunning structure of flying concrete and glass triangles. Before that, in 1949, he built the less-known but equally extraordinary Helen T. and Paul Henry Sheats Apartments, also known as L'Horizon. Helen, an artist, had a hand in the design. The apartments are located a block or two away from Neutra's Strathmore Apartments and, like those, the eight units (now seven, after two were combined) step up the hill on either side of a steep shared staircase. They are also ensconced in nature: Lautner, a protégé of Frank Lloyd Wright, had a passion for organic architecture that echoed Neutra's belief in biorealism. There the similarities end. The staircase at the Sheats Apartments is not a straight shot up the hill as at Strathmore. Instead it twists and winds around a tall, leafy sycamore that looms over and shades the complex. Each apartment is a chunky, yellow stuccoed, asymmetric shape. Some are curved, some more angular. They sit atop and askew from each other,

A dramatic rendering for never-built Sheats Apartments project, by John Lautner

like children's building blocks in a misshapen tower that is about to topple over. This assemblage sits on a podium over a row of cars, whose rear-ends poke out at passersby from their spots in a lot-wide carport tucked under the building. The interiors have few straight walls. Bathrooms are round. Windows are unbroken sheets of glass. Residents have a hyper-sensory experience. Lautner's ensemble is Dionysian compared to Neutra's nearby, elegant Apollonian flats; Baroque to Neutra's Renaissance; an acid trip to Neutra's cool glass of Chardonnay.

It is unusual to find apartment buildings that break so completely out of the box of repeated, standardized units as Lautner did at Sheats. Interestingly, archival drawings reveal that he designed an alternative apartment scheme for the Sheats. It was an oval-shaped tower, several stories high, made of identical planned units accessed off of a central elevator, stacked on top of each other. This would have been quite a disruption in the hills of Los Angeles. It also attests to the longtime push and pull in Los Angeles multifamily living, between low and high-rise.

Sheats Apartments attracted the daring and well-to-do; the actress Zsa Zsa Gabor is said to have lived there. Later, Evan Kleiman, host of KCRW's *Good Food*, shared a unit with fellow UCLA student Blythe Alison-Mayne, the life and business partner of the architect Thom Mayne. Both were smitten with Sheats.

Stunned, Alison-Mayne saw it on a walk, found the manager, and talked her way into an apartment then and there. Kleiman "loved the quirkiness of the place." She had spent a lot of her childhood in a Schindler-designed house owned by her uncle and aunt. "So my aesthetic sense, indeed my sense of well-being, had already been affected by his expression of space, light, and monochrome color palette. The combined Schindler and Sheats experience ruined me for any type of standard apartment and cemented my obsession with architecture forever." Now the entire street has been filled with student housing and several fraternities, which has taken its toll on Lautner's creation. Fariba Ghaffari manages the building on behalf of her mother, Mahin Ghaffari, the owner of Sheats since 1990. She says she is in an uphill battle against the debris, soap, and beer bottles that are constantly being thrown into the shared stairway and fountain, which she turned off because it kept getting clogged with detritus. No one except students will rent there because of the ceaseless noise from the frat parties. She also fights Lautner's impracticalities: most of the walls are simply one three-quarter-inch panel with no insulation. The thin walls, in addition to all the glass, create gigantic energy bills. The radiant heating is controlled from one boiler, so it is a challenge to satisfy the temperature needs of seven households; and, says Ghaffari, "the plumbing system is unbelievable. Pipes surface in the planter." Nevertheless, she says the students love it. They call it the Treehouse.

## Googie Comes to the Courtyard

While John Lautner was building Sheats Apartments he was also at work on another structure that would help shape a new generation of courtyard apartment buildings: Googies Coffee Shop at 8100 Sunset Boulevard in Los Angeles. The futuristic 1949 diner,

with the upswept corrugated metal decking and off-kilter glass window, gave its name to an entire genre of buildings inspired by, aimed at, and intertwined with car culture. They included coffee shops, gas stations, car washes, bowling alleys, motels, and car dealerships, says Alan Hess, author of *Googie Modern: Architectural Drawings of Armet Davis Newlove* and several other books unearthing Googie gems. Googie culture also inspired domestic design: apartment complexes made for easy living, which combined the space-age diner style with new innovations like Gunite swimming pools. "You would have the Googie coffee shops along the main boulevards," explains Hess, "and then on the streets behind the arterial, in places like North Hollywood, especially, or West Hollywood, you would have these apartments with pools. It was an evolution from the motel."

These apartment buildings echoed the Googie-style structures on the commercial strips, with soaring rooflines and sweeping glass windows and kidney-shaped pools, and they found eager tenants. Nichols says that "even at the peak of the single-family suburban surge that transformed the agricultural lands at L.A.'s borders into atomic ranchers and Cinderella castles, Angelenos were keen on apartment living. Endless lists of amenities flood advertising for luxury apartment buildings offering everything from shuffleboard to built-in blenders, screaming at potential tenants to ditch the trouble and expense of owning a home and come join their apartment communities." Landmarks of the period include the suave apartment buildings designed by Edward Fickett that tickled the fancy of many a movie star, such as Sunset Lanai and Hollywood Riviera.

Fickett, born in 1916, was a fourth-generation Angeleno and a friend and one-time employee of Paul Revere Williams; his prodigious output included some

**Sunset Lanai, designed by Edward Fickett**

50,000 tract homes, terminals at the Port of Los Angeles, and Tower Records on the Sunset Strip. He was a fervent believer in modernism who also understood, like Lautner and Schindler, that this architectural language could be easy and life-enhancing, not dour and spartan. Sunset Lanai, on Sweetzer Avenue at Sunset Boulevard, was built in 1952 by a developer named George Alexander. The jaunty structure, with long, slanting roofs, contains twenty-two units in wings of

two stories, with floor-to-ceiling windows overlooking a pool and lawn. Snazzy features include rippled fiberglass siding on the outdoor balconies and Formica countertops with a boomerang pattern. Then, in 1954, he designed Hollywood Riviera at 1400 N. Hayworth Avenue, with thirty-eight one- and two-bedroom units in two wings with angled roofs, soaring upwards, that appear to collide into each other before taking off. The apartments, which were turned into condos in the 1980s, are open-plan designs with lots of glass that overlook a seven-sided pool shaped for play, not hard exercise. "You have a little social life here without really trying too hard," says longtime resident Dale Sizer, an illustrator and fine artist. "And you can be outdoors and have your windows and doors open all year round." The words "groovy" and "pad" could have been invented for this building, which has been the backdrop in numerous TV shows and movies. One of them, *The Oscar* (1966), starring a pantheon of Hollywood luminaries including Tony Bennett, fared poorly before the critics, but inspired a restoration of the building's period sign. When Sizer moved in, the building bore a brass nameplate that simply read: *Riviera*. He happened to catch *The Oscar* and spotted, in a scene of "Tony Bennett picking up broads at the Hollywood Riviera," the original sign in sloping cursive on the building. "So I took a picture of it, and proposed to the board of directors that we should recreate it and keep that classic look for the building because it's so cool." They did, and now, with the continued upkeep of other distinctive features of the buildings, Hollywood Riviera remains a frothy, fabulous fusion of motel and courtyard apartment life.

The building also has lush landscaping with subtropical plants that expressed another fad of the time:

**Opposite: Hollywood Riviera apartments, designed by Edward Fickett**

Dingbat in Beachwood Canyon

Tiki styling. A 1930s Hollywood bar named Don the Beachcomber had kickstarted the fad for Tiki styling, a design phenom that has been excavated in several books by Sven Kirsten. Then thousands of Americans spent the war in the South Pacific and came back with stories of exotic islands with white sands, sapphire blue seas, luscious plants, and radiant women. Apartment buildings now came with lanais, elaborately staged waterfalls, and tropical foliage—banana palms and birds of paradise—dripping down multiple tiers of lava rock. Carved faux-Polynesian wooden and stone statues peeked out from between fern fronds. These places attracted singles or recently divorced people who could sip mai tais and indulge in a more dissolute version of the poolside leisure enjoyed by families in the backyards of new, post-war tract homes springing up across the city. The swinging apartment buildings reflected the constant evolution and innovation in courtyard living throughout Los Angeles. "Los Angeles wasn't simply a story of suburbanites isolating themselves in a backyard in the San Fernando Valley and neglecting their neighbors," says Hess. "There's also this very communal sense of living here."

## Dingbats:
## Stretching Dollars, Squeezing Space

The whole feeling of these postwar apartment buildings could be summed up with the perfect name, says Chris Nichols, "providing it was rendered in glittering plywood letterforms. Taut, dramatic fonts that capture the drama and splendor of 'The Golden Mermaid' or bestow the title of 'Valleyheart Ambassador' on their residents. Ideally they are accompanied by a light fixture or decorative dingbats, shapes that draw their name from the language of typesetters." While the fancy swinging apartment complexes were going up,

so too was a downmarket version with reduced shared space: dingbats, also called stucco boxes. Essentially, they are—per the definitive study *Dingbat 2.0: The Iconic Los Angeles Apartment as Projection of a Metropolis*—two-story, wood-framed apartment buildings, usually constructed on single 7,500-square-foot lots, 50 by 150 feet each. They comprise five to twelve units, which are typically accessed by external stairs and balconies on one side of the structure. The entire front and back of the building is typically lifted over a "soft" underslung, open carport, making cars a feature of the façade, along with the "dingbats," or applied graphics, on their blank stucco street façades: pattern, color, shooting stars, fish, waves, planets, spaceships. These insignia were "baubles and brooches designed to emulate a glamor just beyond reach," wrote architecture critic Mimi Zeiger, adding that they had exotic-sounding names in showy cursive scripts, invoking paradise—Aloha, for example; or pomp—La Traviata; or perhaps a hip nightclub, like the Pink Flamingo, an "exuberantly pink apartment building in Studio City," considered by the L.A. Conservancy to be "an excellent example of the dingbat style." They were mass-produced and proliferated through much of Los Angeles in the 1950s and '60s, earning the enmity of neighboring single-family homeowners and people who missed the bungalow courts they replaced. They have since been elevated to vernacular art status by artists and design cognoscenti, including designer Clive Piercy and artists Ed Ruscha and Judy Fiskin, who are mainly drawn to their street façades. Their plans, recalls a former dingbat resident, Todd Gannon, now a professor at Ohio State University, were typically "perfunctory at best," with open plans and once-modern kitchens, but the graphics

**Opposite: Dingbat on Rose Avenue**

From *Dingbat*, 1982–1983, a series of 2.5 x 2.5 images by artist Judy Fiskin.

put some "func in perfunctory," says Gannon. These apartment buildings can be drive-by delights, especially those that are B-movie versions of Class A modernism, like the Pink Flamingo. However, they were generally not planned to deliver a leisurely lifestyle centered on shared open space. Rather, they were, wrote John Chase, urban designer, in his marvelous book *Glitter Stucco & Dumpster Diving*, "ruthlessly expedient, made out of the cheapest materials, by the simplest construction methods, allowing a maximum number of units to be shoehorned onto a single lot." They were so expedient that the "soft story," supported by slender columns over the tuck-under parking, later proved unsafe in earthquakes. They prioritized the car, reduced outdoor space to a narrow path and shared exterior balcony, and offered tenants views onto the walls of neighboring apartment buildings. The dwelling experience in a dingbat could be as one-dimensional as its façade.

That is not to say residents did not find a home and a sense of camaraderie in dingbats. As thoroughly explored in *Dingbat 2.0*, many did, and still do (notwithstanding the depiction of dingbats as homes for losers in movies like the movie *Slums of Beverly Hills*). To the extent that they delivered an outdoor experience, however, it was generally less intentional and lovely than the earlier courtyard housing centered on open space. Still, the exterior circulation was a sliver of the outdoors. Although the path was narrow, it was still wide enough for a barbecue. When combined with the external stairs and walkways, that outdoor space became a multi-story hangout. And some dingbat builders spent more to add courts or swimming pools or exotic planting out front. Gannon moved to Los Angeles with a girlfriend in 2004, and remembers finding it to be "a kind of lonely place." He was saved by a dingbat in West L.A. with a courtyard and two sets of compatible neighbors. His former home happens to have come with an imprimatur. It had once been photographed by Judy Fiskin. But these shared spaces and vestigial gardens are not integral to the concept as with bungalow courts or garden apartments or today's mid-rises with open roofs. As one prolific dingbat designer, "Packin' Jack" Chernoff, once told a reporter: "Most important is an attractive exterior … We give them the illusion of space. Will cram in as many units as we can. I ask myself, what can I cram on here and still get a nice feeling?"

Dingbats boomed until new parking regulations killed them, too. In 1964, parking mandates were increased so that two-bedroom apartments required 1.5 parking spaces each. In *Dingbat 2.0*, Steven Treffers explains this was impossible to achieve while building enough units to make the development financially viable. As a consequence, apartment builders turned to combining two or more lots on which they put larger buildings with parking fully or partially underground. The resulting jump in scale of apartment buildings, from the mid-1960s on, made the dingbat, in hindsight, seem like a good neighbor in a low-rise neighborhood, and an affordable option in connected living.

**Beverly-Carlton Hotel and Apartments, now Avalon Hotel**

## Sam Reisbord:
## Commercial Modernism with Class

Some designers of apartment buildings opted for a more serious—but no less glamorous—commercial modernism. They included architects well known for their single-family homes: A. Quincy Jones and Frederick Emmons, Palmer & Krisel, Carl Maston, and Ray Kappe. Then there were architects who churned out apartments, like Sam Reisbord. Together with the graphic designer Alvin Lustig, he created the chic Beverly-Carlton (now Avalon), a residential motel, opened in 1947, and the ultra-modern Beverly-Landau apartments.

Reisbord arrived in Los Angeles in 1944 with his wife and two sons after a journey worthy of a Hollywood screenplay. He was born in Kiev, USSR (now Kyiv, Ukraine), to a Jewish couple who immigrated to Philadelphia. When the Depression sapped work opportunities, Reisbord and his wife

Jeanette, a journalist, who both believed in the promise of socialism, moved to the Soviet Union in 1932. There Sam joined the thousands of idealistic architects who went to work with Albert Kahn, the American industrial architect from Detroit who, for a time, advised Stalin's State Industrial Design Trust in Moscow. While many Americans left Russia in the mid-1930s, the Reisbords stayed until 1938, prompting his family to wonder if he had been a spy—at which point they boarded a train on the Trans-Siberian Railway and made their way east. They stopped over in Japan and left in the nick of time, catching the last boat out before Japan joined the Axis powers. The Reisbords landed in Honolulu, where Reisbord took up design work at U.S. military bases Hickam Field and Pearl Harbor, which was then attacked. Eventually moving to Los Angeles, Reisbord took a job with Paul Revere Williams, who was very busy designing stores and elegant mansions, retrofitting the Beverly Hills Hotel and the Beverly Wilshire Hotel, and working on public housing. Two years later,

Beverly-Landau Apartments, designed by Sam Reisbord and Alvin Lustig.

Reisbord set up his own firm and dove into designing numerous structures, mostly apartments and office buildings on the Westside. "My father and my father's friends were all designing apartment buildings for developers," recalls his daughter, Susan Martin—never mind that his circle of friends, which included the left-wing modernist architect Gregory Ain, were avowed socialists. "He rarely designed private residences," she says, "because he found working with people on their homes so difficult. It was such a complicated dynamic that he just stayed away from it."

Instead he worked within the constraints of commercial apartment buildings—"trying to make them as beautiful as possible," says Martin—and created many two- and three-story complexes around a concealed courtyard. He gave the interiors open plans, believing "hallways were a waste of space." Units opened onto the courtyards and shared corridors and stairways. Reisbord's time in Japan had given him an admiration for its architecture and the flattened space of its art, and he elevated the visual impact of speculative apartment buildings by arranging windows, overhangs, fascia boards, shading devices, and wall panels in abstract interplays of verticals and horizontals, solids and transparents, flatness and depth.

At the Beverly-Carlton—a hotel and apartment complex of three buildings at 9400 W. Olympic Boulevard in Beverly Hills, since remade as the Avalon Hotel—gently curving wings wrap around a pool; the structure incorporated tapering columns, vertical fins for shade, and a square wall decorated with distinctive tiles featuring a starburst graphic and asymmetrically placed flower boxes raised over the glass entrance. Opened in 1948, It was cool jazz in concrete and glass. Martin visited as a child and remembers it as "the most elegant place I've ever been in in my life." Marilyn Monroe liked it, too. She took up residence soon after

its opening and, according to *AD* magazine, held onto a one-room cinder-block apartment and continued to pick up her mail at the Beverly-Carlton even when she found more permanent digs. The Beverly-Carlton was a perfect fusion of resort and home.

Reisbord and Lustig also designed the 1949, sixteen-unit Beverly-Landau apartment building on Olympic Boulevard at South El Camino Drive. Two-story wings wrap in a U shape around a courtyard with a pool. The entrance is tucked into the corner. The designers made a Mondrian-like arrangement of modular building elements (windows, wall panels, shades, expressed structural grid). Sadly, the original cladding has been removed, the façade was replaced by a bland, uniform stucco, and a taller apartment building hems it in. The main attraction, the pool, like many apartment pools across the Southland, is now fenced in. Of course, people's safety is vital, but protections like this could not help but cramp the style of this mellow, modern, and quintessentially Angeleno courtyard living.

## Gregory Ain: A Cooperative Vision

Gregory Ain was one of the pioneering designers in Los Angeles in the first half of the last century. Ain, who had worked for Richard Neutra and Rudolph Schindler, was an ardent proponent of mass housing, even though he designed many single-family homes. As a child, he lived at Llano del Rio, a colony founded in 1914 by a lawyer and socialist politician named Job Harriman, east of Palmdale in the Antelope Valley. His father, Max, was a Russian immigrant who was apparently not pleased with Ain's determination to study architecture, because he thought the discipline was "frivolous." So Ain was determined to use his profession to make an impact on society through housing that was modernist in design—flowing open space, multiple sources of

Interior of Rick Corsini's unit at Avenel Cooperative Housing, making the lush backyard feel like it's part of the living space.

daylight, efficiently planned interiors that felt spacious due to the carefully orchestrated access to light and ventilation—and social ideals.

He showed his skill in connected dwellings in 1937 when he completed the Dunsmuir Flats in Midtown: four attached, two-story apartments arranged in a staggered row, and accessed by a shared pathway. On the north, public side light entered from a high strip of clerestory windows; on the south, private side, rooms opened onto a balcony upstairs, and a private, screened garden downstairs. The staggering of the dwellings meant that the rooms had three exterior exposures for light and air, and the outdoor spaces had privacy.

In 1946, Ain designed Community Homes, a complex of houses for a cooperative founded by fifteen members of the motion picture cartoonists union in 1946. The co-op expanded to 280, of which forty or so members were people of color, including the actress Lena Horne. The racial mix, along with the collective ownership of property, was a groundbreaking proposition in many ways, and the group worked hard on assembling the loan and figuring out the plans for the dwellings, which were to be laid out on an L-shaped parcel in Van Nuys. Unfortunately, the FHA enforced racially restricted subdivisions through its mortgage lending and would not change the rules for this project. In 1949, the co-op gave up and disbanded rather than comply.

Ain took his cooperative concept elsewhere. In 1947, ten families contributed $11,000 each, bought a lot in Silver Lake, and hired Ain to create a low-cost complex with a high design that they would co-own, named Avenel Cooperative. One of the co-op members, Serril Gerber, told the *Los Angeles Times*, "We'd seen these modern houses in magazines, and we liked the idea of having a living space that is both indoors and outdoors."

Ain designed ten dwellings that are connected like townhomes along a shared pathway, but, like Dunsmuir Flats, staggered to provide each dwelling with privacy in their back patios. But it had areas for communal living; children played on the walkways in front of the units and in a shared play yard at the back. Inside, space is cleverly organized, with pocket doors, sliding glass screens, and clerestory windows, which all make petite dwellings feel larger. Ain also wanted to break some of the rules of domestic planning, and intended for the kitchen and living room to be on either side of a built-in dining table, so mother would not be sequestered in the kitchen as she prepared food, but instead would be connected to the family in the living room. The FHA nixed that idea and mandated that kitchens be self-contained.

Nonetheless, this was a highly unusual project for the time, given that FHA typically used its loan program to support single-family home ownership, not co-ownership, especially not when the ten owners were dedicated communists. "They would have debates about, 'Should we even allow a socialist in this place?'" says Rick Corsini, current resident and architect of the renovation of three units at Avenel Cooperative, which is now a condominium complex listed on the National Register of Historic Places.

The House Un-American Activities Committee came after at least four of the co-owners, including actor Howland Chamberlain. Serril Gerber was called to testify before HUAC. Ain himself is said to have been spied upon, even by his babysitter.

If anything, the obstacles only encouraged Ain. He next formed a design partnership with James H. Garrott, a Black architect and civil rights activist. They opened an office in Silver Lake, designed by Garrott. Garrott's clients included Loren Miller, the formidable Black attorney who argued *Shelley v. Kraemer* before the Supreme Court. This 1948 case—pitting the Shelleys, a Black family, against a homeowner named Louis Kraemer, who had sued to uphold a racially restrictive covenant in St. Louis—outlawed the enforcement of such covenants.

As for the founding occupants of Avenel Cooperative, they raised their families there, and most of the original members remained there until their deaths, which came at the end of long lives. Every single one of them lived to their late nineties or into their hundreds. Corsini, who has gone on to design apartments and townhomes that aim for the modesty of scale and balance of privacy and common space modeled in Ain's multifamily buildings, points out that the long lives lived at Avenel "run contrary to the real estate industry consumerist model of home ownership where progressively larger properties are bought and sold over a family's lifetime." Perhaps that is because the design so effectively integrated, in Corsini's words, "a seamlessness of form, space, and social experiences."

Opposite: Children play in the shared pathway at Avenel homes.

# 05

# GARDEN APARTMENTS AND THE GREEN COMMONS

Gregory Ain was trying to bring modernism to the masses, through modest-scale multifamily housing for middle-income, progressive Angelenos. Meanwhile, a similar effort was happening on a much larger scale, aimed at people with less money. During the Depression and into the war years, housing costs were out of reach for so many that planners, politicians, and progressive architects embarked on an impassioned effort to house poor and working-class Angelenos. It involved some of the designers of custom houses and snazzy apartment buildings, and they envisioned neighborly living in low-rise, modern buildings around shared parkland—gardens—and common amenities. An ambitious but short-lived program, lasting from 1937 to around 1955, produced almost forty of these complexes, considered by the L.A. Conservancy, which has led efforts to save them, as "one of the largest and most notable collections of garden apartments in the nation." Some were built by a public housing agency, others by private developers with government support. The

latter have fared better over time, but when they were built they all "offered apartment dwellers that same easy access to outdoor living that the modern residents of Los Angeles desired," according to the L.A. Conservancy. This was a vastly scaled-up variant of courtyard living.

## The New Deal Years

Because the devastating Great Depression left millions of people without jobs or homes, President Roosevelt's administration founded the Home Owners' Loan Corporation (HOLC) in 1933 and the Federal Housing Authority (FHA) the following year as part of the massive New Deal. The FHA set about guaranteeing mortgages so buyers could amortize the cost of a house over thirty years, transforming Americans from a nation of mostly renters into a country of property owners—at least, those eligible for loans, mostly white, middle class, Christian people. HOLC created "Residential Security" maps, which graded neighborhoods according to their desirability and intended to aid mortgage lenders in determining where they could make safe loans. The grades went from A: "Newer, Most Desired"

Sunkist Gardens exemplified the common tactic of marketing racial exclusion.

Tent-living on Rose Hill, photographed by Leonard Nadel, 1948.

(color code: Green) down to D: "Hazardous" (color code: Red), giving rise to the term "redlining." Areas occupied by non-whites or a mix of races including whites invariably received a D grade. Parts of Santa Monica, for example, were redlined for the presence of Black, Japanese, Mexican, and other racial and ethnic groups. Housing discrimination was further reinforced by racially restrictive covenants written into the deeds of housing tracts. As a result, many non-white people and the poor found themselves in shoddy apartments or unhoused. Esther McCoy painted a bleak picture in a 1937 essay for *United Progressive News*: "Thirty percent of all dwellings in Los Angeles had no inside toilet, fifty percent had no bathtub, and twenty percent were considered unfit for human habitation."

Two years later, in June 1939, Langdon Post, special consultant to the U.S. Housing Authority and former president of the New York City Housing Authority, toured poorer parts of Los Angeles and, according to a report in the *Los Angeles Examiner*, declared: "Some of

the sections I saw on the East Side make the New York slums look like Buckingham Palace." Waves of people had moved to Los Angeles during the Depression; then they poured into the area for work during the war. The city's overall population jumped again immediately after the return to peacetime and, at the war's end, more than 150,000 families, including many veterans, were living in tents, trailers, and firetrap hotels, wrote the *Los Angeles Times*. For Black veterans, conditions were especially bad. In the early twentieth century, according to Laura Chase, Black people of modest means could buy property in certain areas of Los Angeles and "participated in the bungalow boom." That changed by the 1920s, and by 1945 they were consigned by racially restrictive covenants and other Jim Crow restrictions to living in approximately five percent of Los Angeles. Charlotta Bass, publisher of the *California Eagle*, described in her memoir what many faced: "It was pathetic. Negro families who came to work in the war industries were forced to live in old garages, broken-down storefronts, deserted railroad coaches, thatched tents—all without sanitary conveniences." In the face of all this need, Uncle Sam stepped in to build housing. In 1937, a new U.S. Housing Authority replaced the Federal Housing Administration. It continued the mortgage insurance program for single-family homebuyers and provided loans to local governments to build public housing complexes for lower-income residents. It also guaranteed mortgages for private developers to build apartments for middle-income people. In 1938, the Housing Authority of the City of Los Angeles (HACLA) opened its doors.

Thus, desperate need met a moment of high idealism in progressive politics, planning, and architecture, and all the ideas about healthful modern living that had been percolating for several decades found full expression in expansive complexes known as garden apartments, built on large swaths of land in Los Angeles from the 1930s to the early 1950s. HACLA oversaw the creation of fifteen complexes. They were conceived to house hundreds or even thousands of people, in clean, functional, two-story structures containing townhomes and flats, arranged around grassy courts. Their design drew from L.A.'s popular low-rise courtyard living, but also from the garden city movement, launched in the late nineteenth century by an English planner named Ebenezer Howard, who envisioned self-contained communities that were a spacious hybrid of town and country. They were also inspired by the efficient, rationalist, mass-produced housing concepts of European modernists, and by a new urban planning idea: the "residential superblock," in which multiple blocks of land were aggregated into one "superblock" separated from the surrounding urban fabric by a ring road. This was known as the "Radburn concept," after a new town of that name designed by the influential New York-based planners

Clarence Stein and Henry Wright. The designs were influenced by a communitarian philosophy and the notion that residents should share facilities like meeting rooms, laundries, and nurseries. All this was to be overlaid on the sun-kissed soil of Southern California, whose development patterns already favored garden city living, and still had land to spare.

## Frank Wilkinson and a Dream of Collectivist Housing

After decades of negative perceptions of "the projects," it is hard to imagine just how much HACLA's public housing program initially represented hope, righteousness, and visionary planning ideals—at least as laid out in scholar Don Parson's deeply sourced book, *Making a Better World: Public Housing, the Red Scare, and the Direction of Modern Los Angeles*, about the period of what he termed "community modernism" in Los Angeles, namely modernist architecture put to the service of anti-capitalist housing. This was in good part due to the leadership of assistant director Frank Wilkinson, who went on to be immortalized in plays, documentaries, and even a song, *Don't Call Me Red* by Ry Cooder. Wilkinson had grown up in a staunchly Methodist family in Beverly Hills. In the early 1930s, he traveled through Europe to Jerusalem. He was shocked at the poverty he witnessed on his journey, but was even more shocked at the conditions on his return home, when he was shown downtrodden areas of Los Angeles he had never seen during his cosseted childhood. He gave up on Christianity and channeled his evangelical zeal into providing better housing for the masses. Some said he joined the Communist Party, but according to Donna Wilkinson, his second wife, "He didn't really become a Marxist, just a good Methodist." He was especially interested in public housing, because

"it challenged the very notion of how people lived in America: in isolation, in competition, forever in service to themselves," wrote Eric Nusbaum in *Stealing Home: Los Angeles, the Dodgers, and the Lives Caught in Between*. Wilkinson preached his message by taking busloads of teachers, architecture students, and homemakers, as well as his own children, on "slum tours" of poor neighborhoods. Robert Kennard, an architect who worked for Richard Neutra and Robert Alexander and later designed the Watts Happening Cultural Center, was studying at USC and recalled in an oral history: "[Wilkinson] talked about how architects need to look at social problems more. It's one thing to design things for very wealthy people in corporate America, but we ought to look at what's happening with the homeless and with poor people and with housing…. He said, 'Most of you don't know, but within the shadow of city hall, people are living in abject poverty.' So, on a field trip he took us out, and it was true. Just east of Los Angeles … within the shadow of city hall, I remember he took us to one place where people were living in a garage with a dirt floor, and … there were ten or twelve people living in that garage."

HACLA set about identifying sites and drawing up plans, with teams that included some of L.A.'s most talented architects—including Robert Alexander and Richard Neutra—as well as landscape architects of the time. For many of them, this was a passion project. Several were working simultaneously for affluent clients, though Alexander later told Parson that, following his graduation from Cornell University in 1930, he was "out of work and had plenty of time between ditch digging and an occasional movie set design to think about my 'practice.' I decided that houses for

the rich were also for the birds, and that 'housing' was a vast social and economic problem … and that my professional life work would be more effective tackling these problems." Neutra's involvement with HACLA was also deep, and it was personal: Wilkinson and his first wife, June, even lived for a time with the Neutras in the back apartment at the architect's VDL (Research House) in Silver Lake.

From the start, the effort was caught up in a political push and pull, according to Parson, who spent years poring over community meeting minutes and government housing records. Its very existence was anathema to real estate interests in Los Angeles, who saw the group as an existential threat. One of the lobby's leaders, Fritz Burns, a developer of housing tracts who was as committed to private homeownership as Wilkinson was to public housing, mounted a sustained assault, often through homeowner associations like CASH: Citizens Against Socialist Housing, that Burns founded. Moreover, the new housing was sometimes slated to replace existing cheap dwellings, seen as "slums" by reformers, so the displaced residents were not always thrilled either, even if they got to move into the new homes. Funding rose and fell, sites were selected and then changed in the face of community pushback. Nonetheless, out of the process came ambitious schemes. They had melodious names: Aliso Village, Ramona Gardens, Nickerson Gardens, Rose Hills Courts, Pueblo Del Rio, Mar Vista Gardens, Jordan Downs, Hacienda Village, Channel Heights ….

## MODEL PROJECTS
The first projects off the block were shining models of the idealistic goals of the program. In 1942, some eight hundred families moved into a sparkling new development in Boyle Heights called Aliso Village.

Opposite: Leonard Nadel photographed "substandard" housing for HACLA.

Aerial view of Aliso Village, 1948

Children play at Channel Heights.

Lloyd Wright, son of none other than Frank Lloyd Wright, and Ralph Flewelling of Housing Group Architects created a complex of uniform buildings arranged in courts around shared lawns and parking. Tenants had a baby clinic, a cooperative preschool, and a residents' council. Radical for its time, it was ethnically mixed, and HACLA's official photographer, Leonard Nadel, captured four families—the Taggarts, the Wilsons, the Ramirezes, and the Wongs—as they took up their lives there. As it happens, it was built on the site of a naturally diverse neighborhood called the Flats, home to poor and working class families of many races living in rundown, often ramshackle homes. But to Nadel, Aliso Village was an "island in the slums." It also

modeled the progressive political goals inherent in the housing program; according to Roger Keil, a professor of environmental studies, Aliso Village became a refuge from vigilante violence for young Mexican Americans during the 1943 Zoot Suit Riots.

That same year, Channel Heights opened.

It was designed by Richard Neutra for a hilly site in San Pedro with a ravine in the middle and spectacular views of the harbor. Six hundred housing units were arrayed in cul-de-sacs in rows on a looping superblock. Between each row was parkland. It included a modernist planning concept: pedestrian underpasses at road crossings, separating the foot traffic from cars. "Instead of bulldozing and leveling the site, it was

**Stucco and redwood duplexes at Channel Heights**

treated like a garden," noted Parson of this expanse that was filled at one time with wildflowers. The homes had sliding glass windows and second-floor balconies. There were stores, a crafts center, a nursery and school buildings, a community hall, and a recreation center. Residents met for dances, movies, and town hall discussions. As at Aliso Village, housing administrators encouraged democratic self-management. A resident of Channel Heights named Henry Kraus wrote a chronicle of daily life there, entitled *In the City Was a Garden*, and recalled Channel Heights as a "world of living and striving and learning together." Neutra was thrilled. This was the realization of a vision that he hoped would shape Los Angeles. According to Parson,

in a 1951 article called "Los Angeles in the Year 2000," Neutra prophesied that "our huge urban area will be more 'articulated' into neighborhood communities, each crystallized around a green commons with schools, clubhouse, health center, and recreational facilities."

Three of the largest projects were built in Watts: William Nickerson Jr. Gardens, Imperial Courts, and Jordan Downs. Each could fit large families with units ranging from one to five bedrooms. The architectural language was utilitarian, in a style that has been described as "Minimal Traditional," but they too incorporated principles of openness to greenery, light, and air. Jordan Downs had 700 dwelling units on four superblocks, with 103 two-story buildings laid in rows with grassy courts between them. Nickerson Gardens, which opened in 1954, was the largest, with 1,100 housing units and eight large play areas. It was designed by Paul R. Williams, who had a very successful business designing grand houses with sweeping staircases in revival styles for the leading lights of Hollywood. But he was determined to improve housing options for his fellow Black Americans, who were squeezed into crowded homes around Central Avenue in South Los Angeles. Even though he was a favorite of wealthy white clients, sundown laws kept him from socializing after dark in their parts of town. He lived among Black neighbors and felt their deprivations. He designed the layout to feel homely, not overwhelming in scale. He put a community center in the middle with curving streets radiating outwards, arranged so that from any point residents could only see a few buildings. This prompted the *Journal of Housing* to describe it as having "the feeling of small neighborhoods." Williams added delicacy: recessed doorways and shade-giving overhangs in the mustard-yellow structures. He worked with the landscape architect Ralph D. Cornell and added landscaped greens, baseball diamonds, and fully equipped playgrounds. The housing was aimed not only at the very poor, but at professionals on a higher income. Williams is said to have had great hopes for the project, suggesting that its tenants would live "not just side by side, but profitably with each other."

## Chavez Ravine and the End of the Dream

Nickerson Gardens turned out to be the last hurrah for HACLA's garden apartment construction program, which crashed in the 1950s on the rocks of McCarthyism, lack of support of public housing, and architectural overreach. In 1949, Congress passed the Federal Housing Act launching an era of large-

Drawing of the proposed Elysian Park Heights scheme for Chavez Ravine.

scale "slum" clearance and urban renewal (through community redevelopment agencies). Wilkinson identified a site that he saw as ripe for redevelopment. Little did he know this was "destined to become the most controversial unrealized project in the history of the city," in the words of Greg Goldin and Sam Lubell, authors of *Never Built Los Angeles*.

The land, called Elysian Fields, was in the semi-rural hills of Chavez Ravine. It was occupied by three hundred Mexican American families who owned self-built homes and land where they kept goats and chickens. Yes, these households would have to leave, but Wilkinson promised they would get first dibs on the new homes. He brought in Richard Neutra and his partner Robert Alexander, and they set about designing Elysian Park Heights. It was a mammoth scheme that promised to house no fewer than 3,300 families in 160 two-story townhouses and apartments around cul-de-sacs and parks, and in twenty-four towers, each thirteen stories high. This was part garden city living and part Rush City Reformed, the militantly rationalist, unbuilt scheme with regimented rows of housing in towers and blocks that Neutra had designed back in 1928. Elysian Park Heights had all the hallmarks of this terrifying utopian modernism: optimistic, paternalistic—and brutally indifferent to the actual needs of the existing residents.

Wilkinson and his supporters pushed to acquire the land through eminent domain, but the resident farmers fought back, aided by strange bedfellows: right-wing politicians and home builders like Fritz Burns. In the end, both the farmers who lived at Elysian Fields and the public housing advocates lost, while the wealthy and well-connected won; the residents were forced off their land, but Neutra's housing scheme was not built. A new mayor, Norris Poulson, who rode into town on the fight over Chavez Ravine, put an end to HACLA's building program. He then bought back the Chavez Ravine land, at a bargain price, from the federal government and later sold it to Walter O'Malley, owner of the Brooklyn Dodgers. Meanwhile, Wilkinson was ordered to testify before the House Un-American Activities Committee. He refused to respond to their question of whether he was a Communist, citing his First Amendment rights, and in 1961 was sent to federal prison for nine months for the crime of non-response. By this time, Dodger Stadium was rising from the ground of Elysian Fields. As it turns out, even the project's architects had mixed feelings about the scheme. In 1982, writes Don Parson, Alexander reflected, "Dodger Stadium is a blessing compared to the housing project we designed, and I'm glad we lost."

But it was a loss for the dream of "community modernism." Unloved and underfunded, public housing suffered. More prosperous tenants left when racially restrictive covenants were lifted and the 1968 Fair Housing Act was passed. Tensions rose. Drug

dealing and gang activity significantly impacted the communities at Aliso Village, Nickerson Gardens, and Jordan Downs. The cul-de-sacs became traps. These once heroic projects were now "the projects" invoked in gangsta rap and movies. Punitive design measures did not help, from small but important details like hostile, institutional signs on buildings to very poor-quality structures. Prophet Walker, a developer, grew up at Nickerson Gardens and recalls cinder block walls: "They don't put drywall, and I remember that being etched in my mind, like, man, this sucks. It feels hard."

In retrospect, however, Walker recalls a strong sense of community at Nickerson Gardens. That spirit was vital even during the very bad times. "If someone passed away, you saw people hold each other. Poverty in those days necessitated community, it necessitated human interaction." There were enough kids living at Nickerson Gardens, he says, for a football game at any time, and there was enough common park land for that game, thanks to the garden city plan.

The plan, however, proved to be the undoing of some of the public garden apartment complexes. The design came to be seen as the condenser of social ills, though experts would blame poor construction and management of the buildings, the concentration of poverty along with the lack of local jobs, and lack of agency for residents over their environment. By the new millennium, the visionary housing of the New Deal era had become the new "blight." In 1992, the year of the Rodney King civil unrest in Los Angeles, the Department of Housing and Urban Development (HUD, founded in 1965) approved the HOPE VI (Home Ownership Opportunities for People Everywhere) program to "eradicate severely distressed public housing." The mission included "promoting mixed-income communities" and "changing the physical shape of public housing." Aliso Village was

Jordan Downs, at 103rd Street and Alameda Street in Watts, in the 1950s.

demolished in 1999, to be replaced by a new master planned community, this time called Pueblo Del Sol, designed by QDG Architects. Some residents put up a fight, begging the housing authority to "renovate rather than raze the 685-family development," reported the *Los Angeles Times* in 1998. HACLA said it had no funds for renovation. The lead designer, Ricardo Rodriguez, grew up in a housing project to the east called Maravilla, so he brought firsthand experience. The garden city plan, with its clean-lined worker housing, was replaced with earth-toned structures planned along "New Urbanist" principles: small blocks with sidewalks and apartments and townhomes facing the street, no cul-de-sacs or ring roads cutting the community off

from the rest of the world, and housing types in more traditional styles reaching a mix of incomes. Then, in 2008, HACLA decided the best solution to the travails at Jordan Downs was also to start over. They forged a deal with a consortium of private developers and redesigned the entire complex, with the goal of gradually replacing the seven hundred units with some 1,500 brand-new units of townhomes and apartments, a shopping center, and more parkland, also along New Urbanist lines. The new management was determined not to impose a vision this time around and put an effort into community engagement. Marco Ramirez, with the co-developer BRIDGE Housing, was in charge of outreach but "found out right away that

Cedar Grove, one of the courtyards built in the first redevelopment phase at Jordan Downs.

people didn't want community-building. They were already a tight knit group." Despite its challenges, the superblock had cemented in place a strong community. What people wanted was to work on the vast reconstruction project and to have the right to move back in and not be displaced. Walker, who had grown up at neighboring Nickerson Gardens, wrote the jobs plan, and roughly two-thirds of construction workers have been hired locally, according to the management team. Residents also wanted the shared parks that inspired the previous schemes. "I think when it's all said and done, it's going to be a perfect example of how to execute," says Walker, "and it's all built around greenery and community stuff." As for Neutra's lovely Channel

Heights, it was later sold to private owners who let the buildings decline, and then most of the units were demolished. In his 1982 book *Richard Neutra and the Search for Modern Architecture*, Neutra scholar Thomas S. Hines wrote that visitors still sensed this was something unique. "Amid the squalid ruins of the once-modern village, a sense of place and urbanity remained."

## Private Developers Build the Commons

While HACLA was constructing garden apartments in the face of resistance to public spending on the poor and people of color, private developers were busy, too, creating garden apartment complexes for war veterans and middle-income Angelenos, with partial financing

This greenway is the spine of Wyvernwood.

The central greenway at Wyvernwood

from the Federal Housing Authority. Initially they were restricted to whites only, per the conditions on FHA loan insurance, but that changed and several are now very diverse communities. Residents often express a deep love for these homes, with their access to quiet stretches of common greens within an ever-urbanizing metropolis. But their love can be put to the test since such expansive, low-density developments are a magnet for investors wanting to replace them with

much higher-density complexes. Several, including Wyvernwood, Lincoln Place, and Chase Knolls, have been bought and threatened with demolition in recent years, but small armies of residents have fought back, with the L.A. Conservancy as comrade-in-arms.

## WYVERNWOOD

The first privately developed garden apartment to open in Los Angeles was Wyvernwood, at 2901 East

Olympic Boulevard in Boyle Heights, built in 1939 for people working in downtown and nearby industrial areas. It was built by the Hostetter Estate, an early developer of that area, and designed by the architects David J. Witmer (who later designed the Pentagon) and Loyall F. Watson, with landscaping by Hammond Sadler. On a superblock on seventy acres east of the Los Angeles River, they arranged 142 two-story buildings, containing more than 1,100 dwellings, in courts off of curving streets. The scheme has a central green so long that if you stand at one end you can barely see the other. It is large enough for soccer matches between the many children who live there and for nativity processions, quinceañeras, and other parties.

The first tenants were wooed by the latest fixtures and fittings, including kitchens with two sinks and an ultra-modern Frigidaire. Following the construction of the freeways in Boyle Heights and white flight from the Eastside, Wyvernwood became majority Latino, filled with residents bound by shared culture and roots in towns in Mexico, El Salvador, and Guatemala. At Christmas, says resident Roberto Mojica, tenants dress up and parade throughout the entire place. Such a vibrant rental life has been in jeopardy since 2007, when new owners filed plans to demolish the entire place and start over, reducing the number of units to 4,400 and adding condominiums, stores, restaurants, offices, and new apartment buildings and condos. But occupants, organized by residents including Mojica and Leonardo Lopez, have resisted, with the aid of the Los Angeles Conservancy. Along the way, trees have been removed, causing the sun to beat down on the expansive lawn, which, now barely watered, has turned arid and sandy. Nonetheless, so far the community has stuck together and resisted the development. Mojica credits their fortitude to the strong sense of cohesion at Wyvernwood. It feels different, he says, from the

Children could play and roam safely at Village Green.

surrounding streets of single-family houses in Boyle Heights: "It's more of a town within a big city."

## VILLAGE GREEN

If Wyvernwood was a town, one of the next privately owned garden apartment complexes to open was a village, designed to make you forget that you lived in the epicenter of car culture. Village Green, opened in 1942, sits on sixty-seven acres between Hauser

Village Green

Village Green is nestled into the base of Baldwin Hills

Boulevard and La Brea Avenue in the flats north of Baldwin Hills. It was built by the Rancho Cienega Corporation and was first named Thousand Gardens and then Baldwin Hills Village. It consists of ninety-seven two-story structures and one-story bungalows, containing 629 townhomes and flats, organized in small landscaped courts that connect to a central spine of three sprawling oval greens with picturesque walkways and looming mature jacaranda, sycamore, and olive trees. Cars and roads are confined to the perimeter of the superblock, so residents and visitors first leave their vehicles in the motor courts that form a de facto boundary and then walk into their semi-private idyll. Village Green was designed by Clarence

Stein, Reginald D. Johnson, Robert Alexander, Edwin Merrill, and Lewis Wilson, as well as the landscape architect Fred Barlow. Stein declared the scheme "the most complete and characteristic expression" of his Radburn concept.

For the white war workers and low-income families lucky enough to get spots there, it was a safe and welcoming place where children could play in the large open areas, viewable from the homes and out of danger from cars. Over the years Village Green became very diverse, while trees and shrubs have matured into a resplendent landscape now fiercely protected along with the architecture. In 1973, it became a condominium development, a change that has significantly impacted

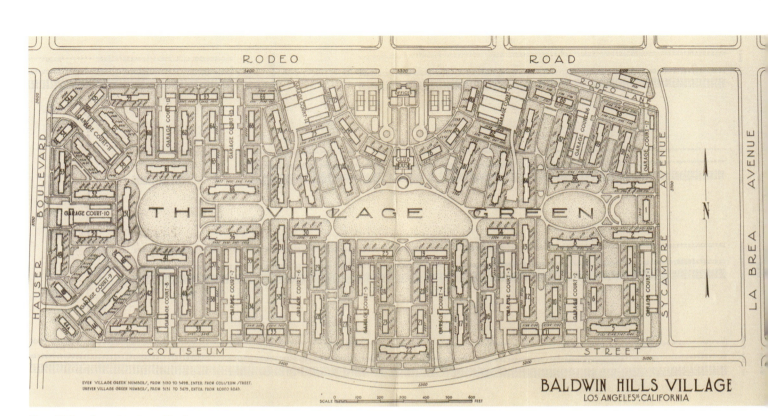

Plan of Village Green showing parkland

its survival through a collective commitment to maintaining its scale and design. Residents garnered designation as a National Historic Landmark; owners work to keep the place immaculate. The condo board maintains 24/7 security and strict control over the exterior appearance of the dwellings—paint colors have to be approved, and only certain types of trees and shrubs are permitted. For a while it instigated a different kind of segregation, banning children, and became largely occupied by seniors until that rule was overturned, restoring young families and the sounds of play in the parkland. It is still moderately affordable. Residents maintain a busy calendar of social events—including picnics and outdoor film screenings—that are open to all, but not obligatory.

Village Green is, in its way, as fantastical a stage-set as the Andalusian courts of West Hollywood, only this time the fantasy is a rural college campus in New England, into which has been dropped a mellow variant of German rationalist housing, with ribbon glazing on façades that are now painted in a select, historic palette of subtle greens, blues, tans, browns, and grays. It relies for its effect on a vast amount of water (said to be recycled) and treatments for its copious lawns. Residents point out that it is not entirely Pleasantville at Village Green; the self-governance, which involves maintaining consensus among owners of 629 units, has its Balzacian challenges. The buildings have some imperfections,

owing to their age, such as poor sound insulation, a no-no in apartment living. But vitally, the dwellings at Village Green have their own private balconies and small patios. "There's enough space for you to not feel confined," says Phi Le Quoc, a resident, adding, "I will probably retire here just because it is that ideal of a living situation."

## PARK LA BREA

In the early 1940s, the first phase opened at what became the largest complex: Park La Brea, just north of the Los Angeles County Museum of Art in the mid-Wilshire area. Ten thousand people live in more than 4,200 units spread across townhomes around courtyards, and in thirteen-story towers, making it the biggest housing development in the Western U.S. and an outlier in the genre due to its mix of scales. The low-rise part of Park La Brea, originally named Parklabrea, was completed in 1944 to a design by Leonard Schultze and Earl Heitzschmidt with a garden design by Tommy Tomson, who also designed the landscapes at Union Station. Tomson is said to have gotten an ulcer from the stress of the huge Park La Brea project. In place of the stripped-down functional style found at Village Green, Park La Brea's townhomes are in a more retro "colonial modern" style. Then, in 1948, to meet a post-war housing shortage, the owners added eighteen cruciform towers. This made it less like a garden city and more like the Plan Voisin for Paris, imagined in 1925 by Le Corbusier. This was a mad but highly influential city on paper that proposed tearing up a swath of the historic French capital and replacing it with concrete slab and eighteen cross-plan towers in monotonous rows in formless expanses of grass. Luckily, the Angeleno

Park La Brea's cruciform towers (left) bear a resemblance to the unbuilt Plan Voisin (top) designed in 1925 by Le Corbusier.
Opposite: Park La Brea, 2022

Postcard of Park La Brea, date unknown

version is more welcoming, perhaps due to the chirpy pyramidal tops on the towers, cheerful exterior paint colors added more recently, and, of course, the sun, which pours into the apartments on two sides thanks to the cruciform plan.

Park La Brea has had its ups and downs, and it appears to have risen in safety and popularity when a new set of owners fenced the whole thing off, making it even more of an island than garden apartments on superblocks usually are. But it is also much beloved. One former resident, Cyrice Griffith, an expert in arts administration, lived there for twenty-four years, raising her son in one of the townhomes around a court that she says was constantly full of life. "You'd come home on any given evening to this quiet community with shady green courtyards and say hi to your neighbors, and somebody would say, 'I'll make the salad … okay, we'll do the fish … okay, we'll bring the wine,' and we had these communal gatherings, impromptu, three, four times a week. It was very special for the kids and the

parents." Griffith says residents joke that Park La Brea is for "the newlywed and the nearly dead" because so many people have lived there for so long. It is also, she says, "divorce central," because both parents can "live in Park La Brea, as we did, and the kids could go back and forth between apartments. I loved it," she reflects. "It really is a village."

## CHASE KNOLLS AND LINCOLN PLACE

After the war came two fine garden apartment complexes by the same architects: Chase Knolls in Sherman Oaks and Lincoln Place in Venice, designed by the partnership of Heth Wharton and Ralph Augustine Vaughn. Both were met with near-destruction and saved by a felicitous compromise. Vaughn was an alumnus of Howard University and University of Illinois Urbana-Champaign, where he studied alongside William Pereira, the prolific mid-century corporate architect who designed the master plan and Theme Building for LAX, the City of Irvine master plan, and LACMA. Vaughn moved to Los Angeles to work for Paul Revere Williams and then set out on his own, becoming, like Pereira, both a set designer and an architect. During World War II, he worked alongside the legendary production designer Cedric Gibbons, who is credited with introducing Americans to Art Deco and Streamline Moderne through his glamorous black-and-white, highly architectural sets for MGM. Then he teamed up with Heth Wharton, and together the pair designed first North Hollywood Manor, then Chase Knolls, both in 1949, and, in 1951, Lincoln Place, the biggest of all these complexes to be underwritten by an FHA loan.

Chase Knolls and Lincoln Place do not have the vast shared greens of Village Green; rather, the dwellings are arranged in mostly U-shaped blocks of

The buildings at Chase Knolls in Sherman Oaks have distinctive window designs.

two-story structures, each cupping grassy courts. The buildings are understated, with flat roofs, stucco façades, and ribbons of casement windows. But each court is made special by its own custom doorway, one overly tall, another with a grid of square windows above, another with diamonds, another with vertical strips of glass. There is a sense of grand arrival, from the street to the residents' pathway to their threshold, with its elegant door frame that perhaps reflects Vaughn's previous immersion in the Hollywood dream factory. The courts are well-proportioned, roomy enough for residents to hold large barbecues, and small enough so occupants don't feel lost like an ant in a vast housing estate. Some units have their own porches and patios. The sense of

individuality is sharpened with different color paint on the exteriors.

Lincoln Place was built to house workers at Douglas Aircraft in Santa Monica, and upon its opening, the *Los Angeles Evening Citizen News* ran blurbs about the modern conveniences in its light-filled dwellings: garbage disposals, built-in breakfast nooks, venetian blinds, Pullman-style bathrooms, laundry rooms with automatic machines, and noise-proof slab doors, all for $63.50 per month. They also touted the twenty-four-acre recreation and shopping area underway nearby that would make Lincoln Place, according to rental agents, "virtually a complete community in itself." Admittedly, this "complete community" was limited

to whites only. Just a few blocks west, on the other side of Lincoln Boulevard, was Oakwood, one of the few areas in Los Angeles where Black Angelenos were able to own homes. But kids there were warned not to go east of Lincoln, wrote a community journalist named Jeremy Divinity, because the Ku Klux Klan was active in West L.A. One wonders how Ralph Vaughn, who was Black, felt as he worked on these projects, which were well-intentioned in many ways and yet barred the many Black Americans in dire need of housing. Today, Lincoln Place too is racially diverse, though less affordable than in the past. It was bought by a development company that tried to evict all the tenants and pack in bigger buildings. But residents fought back for ten years, again in alliance with the L.A. Conservancy. In 2014, the new owners agreed on a deal that would preserve most of the existing buildings and keep eighty-three tenants in place, while inserting thirteen new, more sizable, market-rate, rental buildings in place of ten existing ones, along with a swimming pool and other attractions. Residents of Chase Knolls in the San Fernando Valley went through a similar struggle, and in 2021 the doors reopened, with 141 new dwellings in low-rise structures added to the existing 260 apartment buildings. Owners have perforce kept the new buildings low-key and low-rise, and also had to commit to preserving the very thing that gives garden apartments their Arcadian feel: old-growth trees.

Ken Bernstein, the director of L.A.'s Office of Historic Resources and Urban Design Studio and the author of *Preserving Los Angeles: How Historic Places Can Transform America's Cities*, worked on the campaign to save Chase Knolls and witnessed the appeal of these garden apartments. "The design had fostered an unusual sense of community, where neighbors really did know one another and they encountered each other on the leafy paths under the beautiful trees. The first time I was on that property, you could just sense it was a special place."

The resilience of Village Green, Chase Knolls, Lincoln Heights, and Wyvernwood perhaps attests to a proof of concept for garden apartments. Collectivism was baked into the design of these garden apartments on superblocks. They were intentionally cut off from the surrounding urban fabric, and residents were encouraged to form strong associations. So they did. Says former Lincoln Place resident Li Wen: "The sense of community that was engendered there was evidenced by the fact that the whole community banded together to save it." The cohesion at the public garden apartments was also very strong, but the complexes were overwhelmed by the forces of poverty and neglect. "The idyllic garden apartments that survive (the private ones) and those idealistic ones that didn't (the public ones) stare at each other across an ideological divide that broke, very unfavorably to the latter," reflects Goldin. "These kinds of developments were always on different trajectories, and they reflect the realities of racism but also of a national failure to make housing a human right, which Esther McCoy, Frank Wilkinson, and many others fought so valiantly for from the 1930s on." This fight continues today and has given rise to a new era of "affordable" housing with social space at its core.

A Lincoln Place court, with graceful proportions and threshold

# 06
# COURTYARD HOUSING RISES
## Affordable and Luxury Homes

espite all these social upheavals and architectural shifts, ever-rising land costs, and the emphasis on the car-based, individualist lifestyle, somehow the court system persisted. And in the 1980s it reappeared in an unexpected new guise and scale: in architecturally experimental, mid-rise "affordable" housing built by nonprofit developers, often on arterial boulevards. Market-rate developers followed, birthing a new generation of housing centered on shared open space.

Apartment construction boomed in many neighborhoods in the 1950s, '60s, and '70s, but demand outpaced production and rents escalated. Private developers were now responsible for providing most of L.A.'s housing. Frank Gehry was one of them. Santa Monica mayor Thomas M. McCarthy sent a letter to Gehry's office on the completion of his six-unit building in Ocean Park in 1962, praising him for "an outstanding example of what our free enterprise system can achieve … when the building of our neighborhoods is in the hands of enlightened

**Opposite: Entry to Dunbar Village, in the former Dunbar Hotel.**

private developers and architects who will accept the challenge … to create buildings which not only meet the economic needs of the builder, but also meet the comprehensive housing needs of our population."

Unfortunately, not all private investors were in the business of providing for the *comprehensive* needs of the population. They were in the business of business. Rents leapt up and tenants were routinely evicted. But renters also grew in such numbers that they became a political force, approving rent control in Los Angeles in 1978, a tougher version a year later in Santa Monica, and, in 1985, in West Hollywood. Santa Monica and West Hollywood were in fact shaped by the struggles over rent; a group called Santa Monicans for Renters Rights, or SMRR, became a political force. It endorses a slate of city council candidates each election season and takes positions on everything from sustainability efforts to public education. The battles over rent, coupled with the fight for gay rights, forged the coalition that worked to turn then-unincorporated West Hollywood into a city in 1984. Of course, property owners pushed back against rent control, and in 1985 won passage of the Ellis Act, a state law allowing landlords to evict tenants so they could "go out of the rental business," thereby withdrawing available housing. A decade later, the state legislature passed the Costa-Hawkins Rental Housing Act, which mandated vacancy control, allowing rents to rise to market rate when a unit was vacated (the opposite of rent, or vacancy control, whereby the city could set rents at below-market rates and landlords could not increase them even when a tenant moved out). This incentivized landlords to nudge long-term tenants out—through neglect of their dwellings or other stratagems.

## Nonprofit Developers Reinvent the Commons

Housing options continued to shrink for low-wage workers and the very poor. Into the gap stepped a new kind of housing provider: nonprofit developers of affordable, or deed-restricted, housing, financed through tax credits and subsidized to reach people earning between thirty and sixty percent of the local median wage. These developers started out as small, scrappy, grassroots organizations and have evolved into the primary providers of low-income and supportive housing in Los Angeles. Some were religious in origin, some secular idealists. They include Community Corporation of Santa Monica (Community Corp), West Hollywood Community Housing Corporation (WHCHC), Venice Community Housing (VCH), Hollywood Community Housing, and Skid Row Housing Trust (SRHT), all founded in the 1980s. There are many others.

Some organizations focused mostly on dwellings for working families. Some emphasized homes for veterans or the elderly or people with mental health struggles. Others, notably Skid Row Housing Trust, catered to the unhoused, whose numbers had escalated following rampant urban renewal in downtown Los Angeles and

the loss of thousands of single-room occupancy hotels, or SROs. Nonprofit developers have been extremely creative, seeking sites in unusual places like commercial thoroughfares. They have unearthed dilapidated structures and turned them into housing, some with a great deal of historic charm like the Bryson Apartments, St. Andrews Bungalow Court, or Dunbar Village, a senior community in the former Dunbar Hotel, the jazz-age hotel and club on Central Avenue that hosted the first West Coast convention of the NAACP and counted Duke Ellington and Billie Holiday among its many luminous guests. Several of the corporations were founded or staffed by progressive activists with architectural ambition, who had ties to UCLA's Graduate School of Architecture and Urban Planning. They forged a new kind of multifamily housing for the less affluent. It had visual flair, dwellings with access to light and open air and "community" as a core principle.

The Community Corporation of Santa Monica opened its doors in 1982. It got its start at the liberal Church in Ocean Park in Santa Monica, a hub for social justice in the 1970s under the leadership of a charismatic pastor named Jim Conn. "There was a group of us who were hippie, progressive thinker, community organizer types," says longtime member Judy Abdo, adding that this one-time Methodist Episcopal church in the Ocean Park neighborhood was not overtly religious. Atheists were welcome, along with believers of all stripes. "Jim Conn's vision was like the first-century church, when people were just living their lives, and the church became a part of their lives, but they weren't being just spiritual. That was their life."

In 1978, Abdo, Conn, and a group of members founded the Ocean Park Community Organization (OPCO), a neighborhood block group, to work together on issues like crime and housing. They were worried about the long-term stability of low-income

OP 43 homes in Ocean Park, Santa Monica

renters in Ocean Park, because a mammoth urban renewal project underway at the beach nearby, called Sea Colony Condominiums, was expected to drive up rents. So OPCO came up with the idea of creating a housing corporation that could build in Ocean Park and guarantee lifelong stable rents. Abdo took the concept to the city, expecting to be brushed off with promises of a study. Instead, the city manager and the mayor told them to get started and cut them a check for $16,000. No one in the group actually knew how to build housing, so they turned around and hired Allan Heskin, a professor of urban planning at UCLA who specialized in law and was already active in cooperative residential development in east Hollywood. He brought two other neighborhood organizations, in the Pico and Mid-City areas, into the mix, and he tapped talented housing activist Gary Squier, a student of his who was working on Skid Row, to become the first executive director. Thus Community Corp was off and running. It was, says Heskin, "the first really neighborhood-based, city-

based development corporation."

They got their start buying existing buildings and then began their own ground-up projects, two of which were funded by the developer of Sea Colony. Their first, OP 43, consisted of forty-three dwellings spread in small clusters over five sites in Ocean Park. The goal of the multiple sites, says architect Ralph Mechur, who worked with Marc Appleton on the design, was to avoid a large building and "to break up the massing. Courtyard housing has its own legacy in Los Angeles. And so we looked to that to help us define these projects." So the two architects created modest, two-story structures with pitched roofs, pastel-colored siding, and white painted-wood staircases and trims, echoing local craftsman houses, arranged around petite open courts which are accessed by winding pathways leading from the street.

The ensembles are delightful, and they were published in *Progressive Architecture*, then the most influential architecture publication in America.

Rose Apartments elevates apartments over offices and parking.

Walking past this project, one would have no idea that this was housing for the working poor. That was considered a good thing. Many affordable housing developers tried to keep their buildings low-key to avoid alarming more affluent neighbors.

## Next-Gen Architects; Next-Gen Courtyard Housing

Community Corp next built the Ocean Park 12—two complexes in the same Santa Monica neighborhood, along with another one on Berkeley Street, designed by Julie Eizenberg and Hank Koning. Eizenberg and Koning, partners in life and work, had come from Australia to attend UCLA and were inspired by the social and urban potential of housing. "Our emphasis is about the space between buildings rather than the buildings themselves," says Eizenberg. The Fifth and Sixth Street projects were modest, arranged around small courts, with a more contemporary flavor. Fifth Street had splashes of color and an outside staircase with a sweeping curve; Sixth Street had light-green siding and a rounded roofline. The Berkeley Street project had vivid yellow balconies. In 1986, they garnered a *PA* award. "And then they put it on the cover of the magazine," recalls Eizenberg. After the failures of modernist public housing nationwide, politicians, architects, and planners had backed off of trying to solve the housing problem. "For the first time in a long time, affordable housing mattered."

Community Corp and several other nonprofits commissioned designs that became more assertive, drawing from L.A.'s modernist heritage, the postmodern styling in vogue in the 1980s, and, in the twenty-first century, from the complex forms made possible by digital drawing and fabricating tools. Brooks + Scarpa built Colorado Court at Colorado and Fifth

Opposite: Tahiti Housing, featuring shared bridges, multiple balconies, and a distinctive, colorful façade.

View west of New Carver Apartments by the 10 freeway.

Street in 2002, designed for Community Corp. Its entire south wall was clad in solar panels, sending the message that sheets of photovoltaic cells could be a form of exterior decoration. In 2016 came the Six, built near MacArthur Park in Los Angeles for Skid Row Housing Trust, notable for its bold form, like a giant cube with a huge hole cutaway on one side and above. Their Rose Apartments on Rose Avenue, completed in 2022, put a flag in the ground with three glitter stuccoed wings around open air terraces with views of the Santa Monica Mountains. Its owner, Venice Community Housing, put its own offices on the ground level. Kevin Daly created Tahiti Housing on Centinela Avenue, which opened in 2007. Instead of a three- or four-sided donut configuration, he divided the thirty-six-unit structures into six small blocks, with courts between them and zigzagging bridges connecting the upper stories. An open area at the center of the project is planted with

Crenshaw Gardens, 2019, has affordable apartments above ground floor shops.

thickets of bamboo, irrigated by steep storm water wells. The complex pops in a mix of lime-green and blue-gray with bright orange balustrades. Tahiti Housing is on Centinela Avenue, just yards from the Interstate 10 freeway, yet residents remark on how quiet and peaceful it is in their latter-day variant on garden apartments. The bridges flying through bamboo bring to mind the magical martial arts movie *Crouching Tiger, Hidden Dragon* (2000). "It was definitely an inspiration,"

says Daly, who went on to design more affordable developments in a similar spirit.

There was more. In 2009, the architect Michael Maltzan made a mark with the New Carver apartments for Skid Row Housing Trust, a pinwheel structure in stark white with a stepped inner court, sited right by the Interstate 10 freeway. Then Maltzan designed Star Apartments, completed in 2013, at the corner of Sixth and Maple in downtown Los Angeles. It consisted of

The Arroyo's central courtyard

102 dwellings and a community clinic in modular prefabricated blocks connected like Lego bricks in a kind of reverse pyramid structure. The architect Mark Lahmon put his own spin on the region's founding Spanish Colonial and Mission tradition at Crenshaw Gardens, forty-nine dwellings for seniors built over commercial spaces around a central courtyard in the Crenshaw District. It has arched openings, smooth white plaster, splashes of vivid color, and a decorative steel stair tower that brings to mind the ornamental metalwork at the Bradbury Building. In West Hollywood, the architects Patrick Tighe and

John Mutlow built the Courtyard at La Brea, for West Hollywood Community Housing Corporation. The thirty-two-unit housing complex for formerly homeless LGBT youth, people living with disabilities, and people living with HIV/AIDS, sits on North La Brea Avenue above Santa Monica Boulevard. Passing cars cannot miss its corner, wrapped in swirling ribbons of metal. Tucked behind, out of sight of passersby, is a lushly planted oval court. "I feel like I'm a very rich poor person," said resident Steven Myrick. "You live with dignity here."

Apart from architectural ambition, what unites these projects is common ground. Many of the

**28th Street Apartments. Koning Eizenberg restored a Spanish Colonial Revival YMCA by Paul R. Williams for Clifford Beers Housing.**

Koning Eizenberg added a new residential wing at 28th Street, embellished with perforated metal screens and an outdoor terrace on the interconnecting structure.

affordable housing complexes consist of three to four wings arranged around a central courtyard, sometimes lifted over shops and offices and supportive services. The primary impetus for that arrangement, as with courtyard housing in the early days, was environmental and economical: to naturally ventilate and light the building. The other vital reason was social. In apartment buildings, explains Joan Ling, a former executive director of Community Corp, "There are two requirements. You have to have light and air into every unit, and you can't do that if you have just a box with a double-loaded corridor. So creating courtyards is for the sake of the inside experience as well as the community experience." Gathering spaces were considered vital for

therapeutic reasons, especially for people traumatized by years on the streets, says Wade Killefer, designer of thousands of market-rate and low-income apartments including the New Genesis supportive housing project in downtown Los Angeles for Skid Row Housing Trust. New Genesis features a central courtyard, a shared, grand outdoor staircase, and external corridors. The plan encourages residents to run into each other. "People start to watch out for each other and realize when somebody is late coming home," says Killefer. "And that is how a community is built."

Design teams built in other opportunities for social encounters, like open-air staircases and flying bridges, as modeled at Tahiti Housing. As with courts, they serve

practical reasons, too. Eizenberg explains that at Arroyo, a distinctive 2018 building on Lincoln—white, with flashes of orange and yellow around a spacious court—exterior bridges "offset the need for additional exit stairs while creating opportunity for informal interaction between the ground and upper levels." At Moore Ruble Yudell's colorful 2802 Pico Housing, opened in 2014, kitchens face the court and its bridges so residents have a view of neighbors passing by. MLK1101, twenty-six units of supportive housing for formerly homeless veterans and chronically homeless people, designed by Lorcan O'Herlihy, forms an L-shape around an elevated plaza that is bright with grass and oriented away from the uninviting street below. All the dwellings and shared amenities can be accessed by exterior walkways. Tenants can join each other on the plaza and the terraced steps for Thanksgivings and other events. "I'm trying in a small way to create opportunities for people to gather," says O'Herlihy. "I'm convinced that's where the city has to go." Many of the funders of nonprofit affordable housing development stipulate common space in the buildings they finance.

At some of the nonprofit housing developments, shared physical space comes with supportive services,

**Above and right: A kitchen and shared walkways at 2802 Pico Boulevard Opposite: A screen of resin panel railings, aluminum canopies, and painted galvanized steel tubes in the interior courtyard of 2802 Pico Boulevard.**

Star Apartments has a striking form with its modular construction.

Shipping containers are winched into place at Watts Works.

including therapists and medics. "A lot of times, the people who we're serving in affordable housing have experienced all kinds of challenges in their lives, whether it's financial stress or trauma or other types of physical or mental disability," says Tara Barauskas, executive director of Community Corp. "What we are trying to recreate is the things that give people joy, that peaceful feeling of living in community with others, in a way that really lifts their spirits." Barauskas makes sure to add a community room in all her company's new buildings, and she organizes group activities, like garden days. "Sharing space together and putting their hands in the dirt is what brought residents together," she says. She also created a Residents Council with members drawn from across Community Corp's buildings and, in a forthcoming building, a small business incubation marketplace to foster entrepreneurship. At the Star Apartments on Skid Row, designed by Maltzan, residents have a community garden on an upper terrace. A resident named Bill Fisher described the space as

his personal refuge from the "madness" of the streets outside. "It's like a sanctuary. It's like we have our own private park."

This approach echoes the communitarian ideals of the public housing of the last century. In other ways, they differ from the massive projects in the New Deal, especially in cost. The superblock developments delivered housing at scale, using standardized elements and plans. Today's "affordable" units have become ever less affordable to build due to spiraling prices of land, materials, and labor along with political struggles to get projects built. Each one is custom designed; many involve a battle with neighbors. It can take years to find land and piece together financing, which comes from multiple sources, each with their own demands—demands that sometimes conflict with each other, like different requirements for room sizes. A lengthy entitlement process can involve community

Opposite: Thanksgiving on the shared plaza at MLK1101, built by Clifford Beers Housing on Martin Luther King Boulevard.

PATH Metro Villas in East Hollywood, a self-contained "campus" within the urban fabric, at walking distance to public transit.

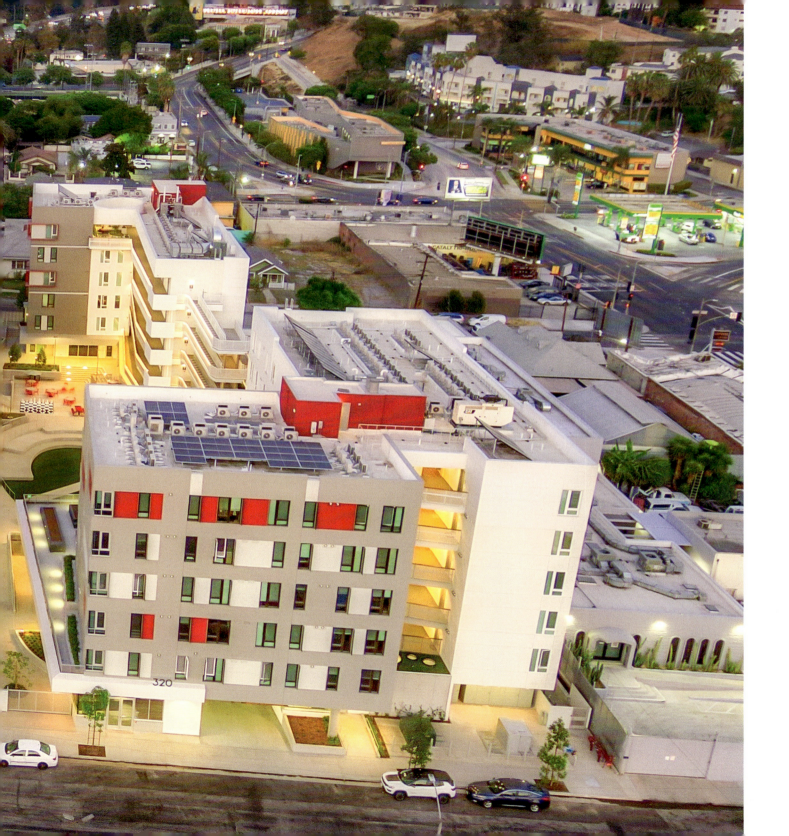

meetings— presentations to a design review board, the planning commission, and the city council—and the production of an Environmental Impact Report. Add to that, sometimes, mandatory parking spaces, which can involve building underground at a cost of tens of thousands of dollars for each space. The upshot is that a small unit of "affordable" housing can cost more to build than market-rate apartments. A project can take years to complete and then deliver a relatively low number of units. Nonprofit developers are now looking at ways to speed up the process and dial back the costs with other forms of construction such as prefab structures, where parts are built in a factory offsite.

Maltzan's Star Apartments was an early test case. In Watts, Daylight Community Development and the architecture firm Studio One Eleven have built Watts Works, twenty-five units made from shipping containers—each one a studio apartment—winched on top of each other with a huge crane. Size also helps reduce costs. Some of today's projects are vast, especially when built near transit stations, where "density bonuses" (permission to add more units in specific sites, like arterial streets or mass transportation hubs) mean they can go bigger and higher, often above shops or offices. PATH Metro Villas in East Hollywood, designed by KFA for PATH Ventures, has 187 affordable apartments and services for the formerly unhoused, arranged in a campus of three buildings around several courtyards; residents navigate the building via internal streets, plazas, and stairways. To live in a building like this is to occupy a small village: like a superblock, but raised several stories off the ground.

From its humble start at the Church in Ocean Park, Community Corp has gone on to manage or build close to 1,900 units across multiple buildings. Nonprofit—and some for-profit—housing developers have built around 118,000 units of housing in the Los Angeles region since the late 1980s. Sadly, however, these projects never keep up with demand. Thousands of people apply for spots in affordable housing complexes; only a few make the cut. By the 2020s, more than 40,000 people were living on the streets of Los Angeles, a seemingly intractable crisis. In 2016, Los Angeles County voters passed the ballot measures H & HHH, a sales tax to fund the construction of affordable housing. Millions of dollars became available. Affordable housing development was now attractive to regular developers. It was also influential. Nonprofit housing developers have shown that people can live on commercial thoroughfares; they have tested new technologies for sustainability and construction systems, which is not always smooth sailing; they have rehabbed seemingly defunct old buildings; and they have modeled a contemporary spin on courtyard living in Los Angeles. Market-rate developers took notice, says Eizenberg, whose firm designs both. "When you start to see inventive market-rate housing," she says, "it's taking some of the invention, both in aesthetic and in terms of configuration, that actually started in affordable housing design."

## Inventive Market-Rate Housing
### WEST HOLLYWOOD MODELS

The City of West Hollywood is so attached to its historic courtyards that it encourages developers to incorporate them into their plans by offering incentives that offset the space given to the court. One of the more influential examples, Habitat825, built in 2007, can be found right next door to Schindler House. It was designed by Lorcan O'Herlihy and his firm LOHA for developer Richard Loring. At a public talk in 2021, O'Herlihy asked rhetorically: "Can you carve out voids in the middle [of a building] and create the

View from upper level of the courtyard at Habitat825.

quintessential courtyard housing project?" He raised this question because land used to be cheap enough that "carving out voids" was no expense to the property owner. Developers today are looking to maximize every inch of their costly sites, packing on as many floors as allowed, deploying a cheap construction method known as "Type V" or "5 over 1 or 2"—meaning one or two stories made of concrete and three to five wood-frame stories above. They don't want to waste square footage on space that cannot be monetized, and a courtyard is no longer necessary for circulation: elevators can deliver people directly from the lobby or parking garage to their apartment floors, and air conditioning replaces the need for natural cross-ventilation and shady outdoor space that a central court once provided. For modern developers, creating a courtyard is a luxury. But it's a luxury some will pay for and some municipalities will demand, because the upsides are so great.

Outwardly, Habitat825 appears to be an opaque, almost windowless façade made of sections clad in charcoal-stained wood and lime-green and white cement board. But a slatted black metal gate is tucked discreetly into the center, and opens onto a terrace that drops down a few steps to an irregular open court cupped by two L-shaped structures, one three stories, the other four, containing nineteen dwellings. The structures, which step back, allowing for open terraces atop units, are clad in cement board and slatted wood balustrades. The style is somewhat pop, somewhat industrial, and couldn't be more distinct from an ornate 1920s design by the Davis brothers or the Zwebells, but the building follows that tradition. The entire composition is designed as a piece of theater, a multilevel stage set for life's small daily dramas, of coming and going, picking up one's mail, taking the dog for a walk—a spectacle for a small group of neighbors.

O'Herlihy had wanted to create social space in buildings since his peripatetic childhood spent on film sets with his father, actor Dan O'Herlihy, often in highly urban cities around the world. He got to try his hand in a string of very distinctive market-rate condo buildings in West Hollywood, built by Loring and shepherded by John Chase, then the city's urban designer. O'Herlihy started with Gardner1050, ten dwellings in a U-shaped courtyard configuration, then designed Habitat825 and Formosa1140.

Formosa1140, completed in 2010, became a landmark of multifamily housing design overnight. The eleven-unit condo building is just blocks away from Village Court, designed by the Zwebells, and is next door to a dingbat. Formosa1140 burst onto the street with a jaw-dropping façade made up of layers of vermilion and burnt-orange metal panels and screens. Beside it is a leafy pocket park. Formosa1140 essentially took the semi-private court out of the heart of the building and put it into the street where, in an unusual twist, it was transformed into common ground for the neighborhood. The development team and the City of West Hollywood came up with a clever scheme: they would transform a portion of the lot into a public pocket park, leased to the city, while the residents would get larger units and private open space on the roof. Chase was so enthusiastic about the concept that he turned up at the city council meeting wearing an outfit in the same vivid hues proposed by the architect. Those colors were an homage to the nearby Formosa Café, onetime haunt of O'Herlihy's father and his buddies, including the actor/director Orson Welles.

In the early years of L.A.'s development, most residential neighborhoods were zoned to allow any kind of dwellings, so single-family houses, bungalow courts, and apartments of all types would sit cheek by jowl, making a visual medley and a lively mix of incomes and household types. Starting in the 1920s, planners became preoccupied with keeping very tall apartment buildings out of residential zones, and consigned them instead to thoroughfares. Later, they pushed for even more extreme segregation of housing types, giving single-family houses their own zone called R1. Lower-rise apartment buildings were pushed to the edges of R1 zones, sandwiched between the commercial thoroughfares and the carpets of single-family houses; renters and homeowners became physically and symbolically separated. Since the aughts, mid-rise housing has been springing up on the commercial strips themselves, often four to five stories of units over a ground level of shops or offices or parking, called mixed-use. These structures offer

**Opposite: Formosa1140 and the public pocket park next door.**

The façade of Fitz on Fairfax features an "art wall" by L.A. artist Cliff Garten.

Los Angeles a new type of lifestyle, one where residents live minutes from a coffee shop or a transit line but also alongside multilane thoroughfares, far from the quiet, leafy streets of the residential zones. The challenge for designers and builders has been to make these places alluring, and sometimes the solution is a lush central court, out of sight of passersby but an oasis for residents.

Again, West Hollywood modeled how this could be done with the Fitz on Fairfax, designed by OfficeUntitled, which spreads fifty-three one-, two-, and three-bedroom apartments into four buildings around a series of courtyards connected by high bridges. The façade, which could feel like an overwhelming and undifferentiated wall, is broken down into a checkerboard of balconies and layered screens and windows that creates a feeling of dynamism and horizontality. This court, hemmed in by a five-story structure, feels more slender and less garden-like than the precedents that inspired it, but still it offers restful open space just yards from a traffic-filled avenue. The Fitz on Fairfax was built by a developer named Palisades that previously experimented with the contemporary luxury court in the very striking Gardenhouse, a rental complex in Beverly Hills that offers an architectural riff on the single-family house and courtyard living.

## GARDENHOUSE

Palisades Development, along with the architect Ma Yansong and his firm MAD Architects, took a bet on changing expectations when they built Gardenhouse, a luxury rental complex with eighteen gabled white structures atop a floor of shops on a major artery: Wilshire Boulevard at North Stanley Drive. Ma Yansong, the architect of the Lucas Museum of Narrative Art in Exposition Park, has offices in Beijing, Rome,

Opposite and above: Gardenhouse inner courtyard and the street frontage on Wilshire Boulevard

and Los Angeles. He is inspired by the style of Chinese landscape painting known as *shan-shui*, and he designs buildings that echo the forms of nature and integrate greenery into their designs. Ma was fascinated with the Hollywood Hills and the houses perched on them. "So we created our own 'Hills' on the flats of Beverly Hills, and added houses on the top," says Dixon Junliang Lu, associate partner at the firm. The design team drove around Beverly Hills, where they were intrigued by the "secret gardens" behind high hedges at private houses, recalls Flora Lee, associate partner at MAD Architects. They created a cheeky spin on the California dream. Homes rise above ground-level storefronts and the façade is wrapped in a "hedge," a green wall of succulents and native plants, created by Seasons Landscape. Atop this conceptual hedge sit bright-white, pitched-roof dwellings designed to look like separate "houses." In the heart of the building is a large, donut-like oval void, ushering light down to the ground-floor lobby. Greenery drips down the sides of the building; a pathway for residents loops around it. The landscaping is highly constructed: plants in the green wall are embedded into a synthetic fabric. Trees and shrubs had to be hoisted onto the roof and embedded in large planters carefully chosen to accommodate growing roots. On one hand, the goal of the design was to create units with a strong sense of privacy—single-family style—so multiple elevators deliver occupants directly from the parking area to their units, and each dwelling has its own private outdoor terrace on the rooftop. On the other hand, residents are thrown together around the oval opening, able to view each other from glass-walled houses across their shared "secret garden."

## MILLENNIUM SANTA MONICA

Many of L.A.'s older courtyard buildings were built on one lot, maybe two. There was a domestic scale to them that made them feel like little enclaves. Modern apartment buildings can take up multiple lots or even a

block and have hundreds of dwellings, like Millennium Santa Monica, completed in 2021. This is a five-story behemoth of 362 units, spread over almost one and a half blocks. It emerged from a challenging process. The site was the longtime home of a trailer park, so when it was bought by Houston-based developers Dinerstein Companies, a group of people paying low rents lost their homes. Housing activists fought to make sure the project integrated some units at an affordable rent, a condition known as "inclusionary zoning." The first pass at the design then caused consternation to the city which, like West Hollywood, encourages courtyards in its housing. The design team had packed the apartments into a huge box with double-loaded corridors. It would

have been a warren of miserable, under-lit units. The project went through several versions by different design teams before landing on the desk of architect Michael Folonis. He figured out how to split up the structure's huge mass into four linear, interlocking bands that zigzag southward across the site, with rows of units lining single-loaded corridors, meaning the corridor was outside. This gave residents windows at both ends of the apartments, bringing in more natural light, and he gave each one a private balcony. The spaces between the intersecting bands became irregularly shaped courtyards and terraces—sixteen of them—at multiple levels, from the ground to the rooftops. The entire composition is a dynamic arrangement of staircases,

Interior of an apartment at Millennium Santa Monica with natural light from several directions.

balconies, and terraces, all opportunities for outdoor encounters. The complex is also bisected by a road into a large chunk and a smaller chunk. In the latter, apartments are closely packed around their court, so much so that neighbors are at talking distance from their balconies.

Residents Lisa Silvera and Jackson Lynch were early arrivals, in 2021, and quickly established themselves as instigators of neighborliness, teaching yoga and planting a raised-bed community garden on the roof. According to Silvera, the day starts with hellos and chats with tenants across the court. It brings to mind the set design for the movie *Rear Window*. However, unlike Hitchcock's classic thriller, in which neighbors

maintain a cool psychological distance from people just a few yards away, at Millennium Santa Monica, says Silvera, they "have formed positive and meaningful connections."

Folonis, designer of single-family houses and multi-unit housing in Santa Monica dating back to the 1970s, says he was not driven by a social idea, per se, but rather an environmental one: that buildings need to respond to their site, to the weather and topography, and reduce dependence on mechanical systems like air conditioning. The goal is to achieve a seamless character between indoors and outdoors. He owes this approach to a group of architects who are pivotal to multifamily housing design in Los Angeles: "I come from the

Above and opposite: Bel Air Garden Apartments, 1948; its courtyard is a surprising delight to those who enter.

old California modernists," says Folonis, now in his seventies, "Neutra, Schindler, Soriano, the list goes on and on." But the consequence of his design approach is that he has created a social condenser, at the scale of a city block.

## The "Court System," Considered

The court was put in the heart of housing as a means to provide natural air and light into the buildings surrounding it. If dwellings were packed too densely on a site this space would shrink, becoming a mere light well. When it was roomy enough to hang out in, it became a hub for residents. It brought to the suburban fabric a micro-urban experience. The framing of the outdoors makes it a focused and usable space, so different from the single-family house floating in a plot of land, with its often pointless front yard. By the time Esther McCoy wrote her seminal 1960 book, *Five California Architects*, the "court system" was, in her view, entrenched in Southern California. As evidenced by the contemporary court buildings, the system holds, despite the cost of land and the new technologies that might obviate its existence, and various municipal codes—such as fire and access and, of course, parking— that can work against them. They appeal because

they satisfy some primal needs, perhaps starting with safety. One of the multifamily apartment dwellers who attested to this was Misti Plante, a resident of Bel Air Garden Apartments, designed by architect A. Quincy Jones. The mid-century complex has nine units on two stories around an oval court with a pond in the middle. It is cocooned from the world, accessible and visible from the street only via a small, decorative metal gate. To lovers of mid-century modernism, this building is admirable if in need of an upgrade. Its cedar wood has been painted a dull gray-green. To Plante, whose husband was traveling a lot for work, it represented protection. Her two daughters played in the central court, sequestered from the street and traffic. She had previously lived in a single-family home by herself, in Malibu. "And I was constantly scared," she said. "My neighbors are a huge part of me feeling safe, and they've become a huge part of our family."

McCoy used the word "system" presumably to infer that courts are stitches knit into the fabric of the city. "For people living around the courtyard, the space provides a sense of safety and privacy," say the architects Lawrence Scarpa and Angela Brooks. "The courtyard is a quasi-public space that mediates between the home and the street. For the city at large,

the courtyard is an urbane housing type that fits well into neighborhoods." At their architectural best they are handsomely arranged, inviting residents on a clear procession through space from the public realm—the street—to the semi-public—the walkway or court— to the threshold of the resident's unit—a porch or doorstep—and finally into the private realm—the interior. Procession, notes architect Michael Lehrer, is one of "the fundamental attributes of home and probably among the most important providers of a sense of grace and graciousness."

That is not to say that all courtyard housing succeeds. If the court is ill-proportioned—too dark, too narrow, or too large relative to the buildings around it, it can be unwelcoming. If the building is spartan and the court devoid of greenery, it can feel institutional. If it doesn't strike the right balance of privacy and public space, it can certainly fail. A long-term resident of a Santa Monica bungalow court said the intense neighborliness of her court—her daughter met her lifelong best friend there—was also off-putting, because residents were always in each other's business. This could have been because they shared ownership of the property, so they had to be in each other's business, or perhaps it was because her court dwellings did not have their own private outdoor space, a place of personal refuge which appears to be key to the success of communal life. As Gehry said about the Hillcrest Apartments, his goal was for the court area to give tenants a sense of "peripheral connection," a subtle sense of a reassuring human presence, while giving each tenant a private balcony.

The peripheral connection Gehry refers to is between residents within a building. But there is another visual relationship that buildings have: between home and the street. Courtyards in Los Angeles come wrapped on one, two, three, and four sides, and the dwellings typically look onto the court. When the building is four-sided, or has three sides with a fence or wall on the fourth side, the building is essentially turning its back to the street. This has been described by some planners and designers as "introverted" or "protectionist" or "defensive." Even courtyard housing evangelist Stefanos Polyzoides and his co-authors have written that by "drawing the life of the city away from the sidewalk, and the street and inside the courtyard," such apartment buildings generate a "sense of anonymity and dissociation from the urban fabric."

In the 2020s, a good number of apartment buildings springing up on the region's arterials are being designed with courts, windows, or balconies positioned to give residents a view directly onto the street. The idea is that residents will enjoy a lively urban experience, especially if they are above shops and coffee bars. How pleasant to sit on one's balcony and watch the world go by. This would be pleasant if there was a lively urban scene to view. But on the arterials—or, even worse, by the freeway—where many of these new structures are going up, the street scene can be several lanes of noisy cars spewing out car exhaust. Moreover, the outward-facing arrangement means that passers-by can watch the residents, which can create a feeling of vulnerability. Brooks + Scarpa came up against those feelings when the firm designed the Six for the nonprofit developer Skid Row Housing Trust. The Six is near MacArthur Park in the Westlake neighborhood of Los Angeles. It has fifty-two apartments and studios for formerly homeless individuals. A third of its permanent supportive housing is aimed at veterans. That's where the name came from; in the military, "got your six" means "I've got your back." Angela Brooks and Larry Scarpa designed a bold-looking building around a court that opened directly towards the street. But then they met

The shared courtyard at The Six is raised off the ground, offering tenants both prospect and sanctuary.

with a building committee that asked for the court to be raised off of ground level and over a first floor of supportive services. From there, residents can look over onto the sidewalk, but it's not a direct link. Brooks said the design is better for it. "It's more of a refuge for the tenants, so the tenants themselves feel more protected by the building and by the space of a courtyard."

But courtyard housing is not the only prototype for a Los Angeles lifestyle centered on coexistence. There

is another typology, one that comes with gyms, spas, and dog runs. It is rooted in a Los Angeles multifamily housing type that seemed like a short-lived East Coast import: the luxury apartment–hotel.

# 07

# FROM THE APARTMENT-HOTEL TO LUXE LOFT LIVING

While many Angelenos dream of a single-family house, there are others who would rather rent in a well-managed building. This includes the young and the elderly, and those not interested in yard work. For these people, what could be better than a grand, serviced apartment-hotel? This was a type of residence borrowed from the East Coast, but it flourished in Los Angeles, a magnet for tourists, adventurous singles, and people dropping in for short-term projects like making a movie. In the Southern California climate, such buildings could offer outdoor attractions like rooftop bars, spas, and swimming pools—catnip for the fashion and entertainment community, for whom posing by the pool is practically a job. From a social perspective, such dwellings were perfect for temporary residents, who unpacked their bags, went to the bar, and found instant company. At their most luxurious, apartment-hotels were opulent and catered to every whim, but aspects of the lifestyle they offered—the rooftop pool, a doorperson, gyms—have trickled down to loft-living

**Opposite: Roof terrace of Eastern Columbia building, following adaptive reuse and addition of a pool.**

today, in retrofitted industrial buildings, as well as newly built faux "loft" complexes in downtown, the Arts District, Hollywood, and beyond.

## The Roaring '20s

The popularity of apartment-hotels exploded in tandem with the movie industry, and their designs embraced its love of fantasy. Following the construction of the Bryson in 1913 (see page 32), towers of four to thirteen stories went up on and near Wilshire Boulevard in Westlake and the Wilshire-Ambassador district around the Ambassador Hotel, the now-demolished, legendary society watering hole. Apartment-hotels were built in architectural styles evocative of castles and manors in old Europe, yet replete with modern creature comforts like elevators and neon signs beaming from their roofs.

The Gaylord (1924) and the Asbury (1925) were particular jewels. They boasted high ceilings, elaborate plasterwork, and grand social spaces, like ballrooms and restaurants. Adolfo V. Nodal, former general manager of the Los Angeles Cultural Affairs Department, spent many years living and mingling with neighbors in

El Royale was the epitome of New York-style living, with California-style access to a private club and golf course.

the Asbury and the Ansonia, and "it wasn't just, get up in the morning, go to work, and come back," he recalls. "They weren't just sleeping places, they were places to spend time in." Nodal also led the restoration of the luminous rooftop signs. Once neon appeared in Los Angeles in the early 1920s, it fast became "a symbol of modernism," he says, and the cluster of them in the Wilshire corridor "really created a sense of place." The sight may have captivated the journalist and civil rights activist Oswald Garrison Villard. On visiting Los Angeles in 1923, he described the cityscape of "innumerable homelike stucco or wooden bungalows, small and crowded but often attractive in their architecture and delightfully landscaped," while

"its skyscrapers, scattered through the city, stand by themselves like great and beautiful towers."

Apartment-hotels spread to Hancock Park. On Rossmore Avenue at Beverly Boulevard, Country Club Manor was built by Leland A. Bryant in 1926; William Douglas Lee created the sumptuous El Royale in 1929, and Max Maltzman designed the Ravenswood for Paramount Pictures in 1930. They all looked onto the exclusive Wilshire Country Club, where actors and businesspeople could mingle over leisurely games of golf. El Royale was an exuberant fusion of Spanish Colonial Revival, French Rococo, and Renaissance styles. Inside were gleaming marble floors, elaborate chandeliers, and hand-carved joinery. When the

The Sunset Tower (right) is near a contemporary luxe residential hotel, the Pendry Hotel and condos (center), designed by EYRC Architects with Martin Brudnizki.

powerful talent agent Kevin Huvane moved from New York to L.A., he took up residence in El Royale, bringing a circle of glitterati for a period dubbed "the reign of Huvane." The popular Southern California TV host Huell Howser lived there from the 1980s until his death in 2013. The jazz age saw the construction of the Art Deco Ravenswood, with streamlined glamor: unadorned pilasters, chamfered door frames, and a grand lobby with terrazzo floors and lofty, double-height ceilings. One of its first tenants was the sassy actress-writer-singer Mae West, who took up residence in the penthouse, #611, when the building opened and lived there until her death in 1980. Numerous stories surround West's stay at Ravenswood: among them, that

she held seances in her apartment, and got into a fight with the owners because they would not permit entry for her Black boyfriend, boxer William Jones.

Further west in Beverly Hills, was the Beverly Wilshire Apartment-Hotel, which opened in 1928. Real estate developer Walter G. McCarty hired the architectural team of Walker & Eisen to design the building with both apartments and hotel suites. In the 1940s, architect Paul R. Williams remodeled the structure which by then had become primarily a hotel. After a huge tower designed by Welton Becket & Associates was added to the rear in 1971, the Beverly Wilshire Hotel was sealed in L.A. lore by its depiction in the film *Pretty Woman* (1990) and by residents such as

View of Chateau Marmont from the west

Warren Beatty, who spent fifteen of his bachelor years holding court in a palatial suite in the newer building.

Apartment-hotels, towers of opulence, flourished on the Sunset Strip. The 1929 Sunset Tower was designed by Leland A. Bryant. Bryant, known for working in the so-called Châteauesque style, ditched the pomp and Mansard roofs of sixteenth-century French palaces for fifteen stories of reinforced concrete—a first—in stepped-back Zigzag Moderne with an elaborate plaster frieze of plants, animals, zeppelins, legendary creatures, and Adam and Eve. Sunset Tower was initially composed of apartments, with large windows offering spectacular views and modern conveniences like outlets in every bathroom for electric shavers. Marilyn Monroe, Errol Flynn, Elizabeth Taylor, Frank Sinatra, and even gangster Bugsy Siegel are said to have spent time there. One habitue, John Wayne, reportedly brought a cow up to his penthouse, telling late-night guests that if they wanted cream in their coffee, they could get it from the source. When the Sunset Tower fell on hard times in the 1980s, it almost became condos, then was turned into a luxury hotel called the St. James's Club whose members included David Bowie. Later it was known as the Argyle and finally, at least for now, the Sunset Tower Hotel, owned by Jeff Klein and fully revamped in discreet elegance by interior designer Paul Fortune. Fortune says that to create glamorous but comfortable interiors, creamy tablecloths are a must—"they soften the diner's immediate environment"—and cold whites, primary colors, and spotlights are *verboten*. In his view, these "make you look like the Bride of Dracula."

If the beautiful people wanted somewhere really louche to stay, they could decamp to Chateau Marmont, which opened on Sunset in 1929 as an apartment building and became a hotel. The Châteauesque idyll tucked behind a tall hedge was designed by William Douglas Lee and Arnold A. Weitzman. Later, the owners added some Spanish-style cottages, and bungalows designed by Craig Ellwood. "The hotel was typically so quiet," noted the writer Quentin Crisp in an essay he wrote for the *New York Times* in 1982, "that you understand at once how it wrung praise even from the marmoreal lips of Miss Garbo, and why for years Mr. Howard Hughes maintained a suite there. Why didn't these two hermits marry and take over the whole building?"

## 1950s Brutalist Glamor: Wilshire Terrace

Many of the luxe apartment-hotels fell out of fashion during the Depression and the war years, becoming faded old dowagers available at rents regular citizens could afford. But even as Los Angeles entered its Eisenhower years, with the G.I. Bill enabling the growth of suburbs and nuclear family life, the amenity-filled tower still exerted an allure. In 1958, business and civic leaders attended the opening ceremony of Wilshire Terrace, a fourteen-story tower designed by another Austrian modernist architect, Victor Gruen. It was designed in a bracingly brutalist style.

Wilshire Terrace was one of the first luxury towers to put down anchor on the snaking stretch of Wilshire Boulevard that runs from Westwood to Beverly Hills, nicknamed Condo Row or Platinum Mile. It sits at the corner of Beverly Glen Circle and Wilshire, next to Holmby Hills, and beside the Los Angeles Country Club. The hilly area was dotted with period-revival private houses. Into this oasis of quiet affluence descended the New York developer and construction manager Norman Tishman, who was confident there

Wilshire Terrace, facing Wilshire Boulevard

The private pool and other luxury amenities at Wilshire Terrace were only visible to residents.

was a market in Los Angeles for another kind of luxury living: high-rise multifamily buildings, but with the desirable attributes of a Southern California house: privacy, ownership, convenience for the automobile, and outdoor space. Tishman reached out to Victor Gruen, a motor-mouthed, idea-a-minute, Austrian-Jewish émigré and head of an influential planning and design firm in Los Angeles. In 1956, Gruen designed the culture-changing Southland Mall near Detroit. This was America's first fully covered suburban shopping destination. Under one roof, the 75,000 shoppers on opening day could find ten acres of stores and a court with a goldfish pond, birds, and art. *Time* magazine described it as a "pleasure-dome-with-parking."

Now Gruen set to work rethinking another building type. He, his partner in charge of design, Rudi Baumfeld, and Tishman created Wilshire Terrace, a fourteen-story residential tower containing 112 dwellings with four to eight rooms each, as well as five penthouses. The Gruen building was innovative

in many ways. It broke the thirteen-story height limit in effect up to that time, and it was the first multistory L.A. apartment building where residents could own their units, in a cooperative arrangement. Promotion for the building reassured potential investors, who had to buy their dwelling outright, that "the wise selection of tenant-owners assures congeniality of outlook and purpose." It was technologically very advanced, with full air conditioning in each unit and a concrete frame structure with double-stud walls for optimal soundproofing. There were several sets of service and passenger elevators, so that residents could ascend to their dwelling with barely an encounter with neighbors or staff, though they could choose to gather with neighbors at the poolside. Finally, it offered a dramatic new take on indoor-outdoor living: each unit opened onto a private, double-height, seventeen-by-eighteen-foot balcony, complete with its own outdoor fireplace—essentially an outdoor room.

The resulting inside-outside effect was enhanced by the units' glass walls. At least, that is what was recommended by the designers in early drawings. In later years, some residents chose to wall in the outside area, so as to create more indoor square footage, or they lowered the outdoor room's ceiling height with canopies to cut out glare from the sun. Ken Weiss, president of the Wilshire Terrace Cooperative board, kept the double height and is an admirer of the ingenious design. He and his wife, Cathy, purchased two units in Wilshire Terrace after many years residing in a custom-designed home in tony Trousdale Estates in Beverly Hills, which "took a huge amount of upkeep to keep it really pristine." For him, the connection to the outdoors, without the landscape maintenance, is one of the main attractions of the building. Standing with Weiss on his fourteenth-floor, south-facing balcony-room, taking in the 180-degree view of Los Angeles, is a dramatic experience. It was probably even more dizzying when Wilshire Terrace first appeared.

Wilshire Terrace precipitated construction of a flurry of high-rise condos on the stretch of Wilshire Boulevard between Westwood and Beverly Hills. At the time it was built, the structure loomed over expanses of flat land. There was only one other tall apartment building nearby: the ten-story, salmon-colored 10401 Wilshire on the other side of Beverly Glen, designed in 1951 by Martin Stern Jr. Next to Stern's soft-pink structure and the villas on Beverly Glen, Wilshire Terrace must have looked shockingly tough, striking in the muscular way of the 1952 Unité d'Habitation in Marseilles, Le Corbusier's extraordinary rough-cast concrete (*béton brut*) slab containing apartments, hotel, eateries, and shops.

Wilshire Terrace's visual impact lies in the layered, abstract arrangement of deep-set balconies intersecting long balustrades, the vertical exposed structure, and square planters. The planters, originally coated in vermillion glass tiles, popped with primary color against the layers of gray. The red planters, incidentally, were an homage to Frank Lloyd Wright, who signed his drawings with a red square. This detail was chosen by Gruen project leader Ben Southland, a devotee of Wright's work. That's according to Frank Gehry, who worked for Gruen at the time. Sadly those tiles have gone, casualties of a fire that badly damaged Wilshire Terrace in December 1989, though the building was since restored by Gruen Associates.

Upon Wilshire Terrace's opening, on January 29, 1959, the *Los Angeles Times* referred to it as "Norman Tishman's $13 million monument to luxury living." Residency came with valet service, massage rooms, and a lavish, marbled lobby. The units sold quickly; one early resident was Billy Wilder, the director whose hilarious film *Some Like It Hot* came out the year Wilshire Terrace

Luxury towers by arterials with a garden over parking are now commonplace; Metropolis, 2018, designed by Gensler, is an example.

opened its doors. *Progressive Architecture* magazine raved about the building, saying it combined the livability of a private home with the convenience of a first-class hotel. However, David Gebhard and Robert Winter, authors of *An Architectural Guidebook to Los Angeles*, were not impressed. They listed Wilshire Terrace simply as one of a "double wall of expensive condo buildings" that have had a "devastating" effect on the single-family communities that surround them. Implicit in their critique is the notion that detached single-family is the natural and correct mode of housing for Los Angeles, and that towers have rudely invaded their space. Now that endless houses on large lots are understood to be an inefficient use of resources, this is a harder argument to make. Having said that, Wilshire Terrace was in its own way a product of the car city. It was a Manhattan-style development that did not come with a Manhattan lifestyle—walkability and mass transit. Buried underneath a capacious garden at the rear of the site is a huge parking lot, concealed from view by a

The lobby of the Mondrian in West Hollywood, designed by Philippe Starck for Ian Schrager

retaining wall made of a mid-century favorite, lava rock. Moreover, in keeping with the modernist planning ideas of the time, which favored buildings standing alone in an expanse of parkland or parking, the tower was set back from the street, with a walled-in pool and outdoor lounge in front. Residents dropped their cars with a valet in a porte-cochère at the back of the building and entered the lobby from there. The building had no streetfront entrance; it did not invite pedestrians.

The Wilshire Terrace tower has proven prescient, however, as luxury housing developers today endeavor to create an indoor-outdoor experience for dwellers living many stories off the ground; its garden over parking is a precursor to the multi-tier "parking podiums" with park areas and dog runs atop, which are part of today's high-rise luxury towers.

## Boutique Hotels, Boutique Lofts

Developers continued to build luxury apartment buildings, especially in old residential areas that had been deemed "blighted" by planners and politicians, and were now being aggressively redeveloped through "urban renewal" projects like those on Bunker Hill and at Santa Monica Shores. In fact the crusty writer Charles Bukowski, who spent many years living in a small apartment on De Longpre Avenue in East Hollywood, noted crossly in 1967: "And there is another high-rise apartment going up directly across the street. I am now

The Standard boutique hotel on Sunset Boulevard, 2000. The hotel closed in 2021.

completely surrounded. I see all these beehives. Luckily I can't afford to die in such voluptuous candy shit; I will end up in a cardboard box in the hills." But the highly stylish apartment-hotel hybrids seem to have lost steam in the post-war period, until the appearance of boutique hotels. This new wave of hostelries, aimed at the mobile, creative set at mid-range prices, appeared in the 1980s when Ian Schrager started applying the principles of a great nightclub to hotel design. They wound up having a huge influence on multifamily housing centered on active social spaces.

Ian Schrager was the cofounder of the legendary 1970s discotheque Studio 54 in New York. He subsequently went to prison for fraud, then reappeared

and opened three game-changing hotels, with design by French *enfant terrible* Philippe Starck: Morgans, the Royalton, and the Delano. The duo then barnstormed Los Angeles and transformed the Mondrian on Sunset Boulevard, originally built as an apartment building in 1959. They added fifty shades of white—paint, fabric, carpet, accessories—and a James Turrell light installation, plus decor that looks straight out of the Mad Hatter's tea party. "Everything is off-balance," wrote *Los Angeles Times* architecture critic Nicolai Ouroussoff, when the Mondrian opened to great fanfare in 1996. "At the windows, pale white curtains reach only part way down to the floor like dwarfish stage props, and 'game chairs' have chess or backgammon

The Toy Factory lofts' lobby features an adapted shipping container.

tables sprouting out of their arms." A live model writhed in a tank in the lobby. A rooftop bar and pool amid cabanas and plants in oversized pots made everything seem upside-down and surreally delicious.

Other hoteliers copied Schrager: André Balazs with the Standard hotels, one on Sunset Boulevard in a converted mid-century apartment building, and another in downtown Los Angeles in a retrofit of a 1960s office building, to which he added table tennis, a rooftop pool, and oversized beds and baths for basketball players playing at Staples. Interior designer Kelly Wearstler entered the picture, launching a glittering career in hotel and domestic design with hotspots like the Avalon (formerly the Beverly-

Carlton), Maison 140, and Viceroy hotels. ACE hotels appeared, in Palm Springs and in Downtown Los Angeles (DTLA) in a restored and adapted United Artists Hotel on Broadway. In all these places, idiosyncratic design, changing art installations, and in-house DJs in the reception areas and on the roof terraces were the name of the game. Hotels live or die on the power of their lobbies, said Schrager at the 2019 opening of the West Hollywood Edition, a hotel chain for which he became a consultant. They had to feel "like a gathering place." The boutique hotels emerged at the same time as a newly named demographic: the so-called "creative class." Writers, filmmakers, designers, arts workers, tech start-up founders … this new breed of white-collar workers were drawn to the boutique hotels. Residential developers took notice.

The Standard hotel in DTLA, opened in 2002, had taken advantage of the Adaptive Reuse Ordinance (ARO), a piece of legislation passed in Los Angeles in 1999 that would permit the conversion of defunct commercial buildings for new uses like hotels and live-work housing. The genius of the ordinance was to lift the usual parking mandates. This unleashed a development gold rush, drawing thousands of new residents to downtown and turning the historic Old Bank District and the Arts District into centers of market-rate loft living. It was a dramatic turnaround for the once thriving downtown that had emptied out since the construction of the freeways and white flight to the suburbs. There were knock-on effects, however, as SROs and old apartment buildings that served Skid Row were bought and rehabbed into housing for the affluent. Generally, though, ARO, which created thousands of homes in existing structures—without the cost and carbon footprint of new construction and hassles associated with building in residential neighborhoods—has been seen by policymakers and planners as an urban renewal success story.

In the early days of adaptive reuse in DTLA, loft conversions were fairly basic until developers, seeing the crowd hanging out beside the rooftop pool of the Standard at Sixth and Flower, in the staid Financial District no less, realized prospective loft-dwellers might like this amenity, too. Killefer Flammang Architects (KFA) worked on the adaptive reuse of the old Pacific Electric Building—the offices and depot for Henry Huntington's Pacific Electric Railway line—and the glorious aquamarine Art Deco Eastern Columbia Building (in collaboration with designer Kelly Wearstler). At both, they strengthened the roof and added a shimmering pool. The two projects opened in 2005, when a pool on the roof of a retrofitted old office building was an innovation. Karin Liljegren, who worked at KFA during that time and went on to remodel numerous downtown buildings with her firm Omgivning, says, "Today, you have to have a pool on your roof if you're doing it right."

As a rooftop pool became standard-issue, property owners added other enticements, installing dog runs and gyms and in-house barber shops and ground-floor coffee bars, in an escalating game of amenity one-upmanship. It was the boutique hotel effect. In 2006, the development company Linear City unveiled their retrofit of the Toy Factory, a seven-story steel-and-concrete warehouse turned air raid shelter turned toy factory in the Arts District. This was one of the early loft conversions in the industrial area east of Alameda Street and Little Tokyo that for several decades had served as home to artists able to pay a peppercorn rent in minimally converted warehouses. The area was taking off, especially since the 2001 arrival of the Southern California Institute of Architecture, or SCI-Arc, which moved into the former Santa Fe Freight Depot, a 1907 building that, at 1,250 feet in length, was as long and slender as the trains it once serviced. Toy Factory was designed by Clive Wilkinson Architects. The team put a shipping container into the lobby as a place where people could get their mail and mingle. Residents could enjoy a rooftop pool, semi-private cabanas, and summer evening potlucks. Sean Knibb, a landscape and interior designer, added artful installations of grasses, succulents, and scented geraniums in planters made of very wide industrial drain pipes on one of its roof terraces. Outdoor barbecuing had come a long way from a backyard in the San Fernando Valley. The *Los Angeles Times* enthused about movie screenings "on an infinity deck with drop-dead skyline views, and a fireplace for hanging around on cool California evenings."

On the rooftop of the Toy Factory, the swimming pool takes the hard edge off loft living in the industrial Arts District

# 08

# GOING BIG ON CREATING A COMMUNITY

## One Santa Fe

As the supply of convertible older buildings dried up, new, ground-up construction took over in South Park and the Arts District. In the aughts, a conglomerate of developers signed a deal with L.A. Metro to build housing on Santa Fe Avenue parallel to SCI-Arc. One Santa Fe Partners and McGregor Partners brought in Michael Maltzan, designer of housing for Skid Row Housing Trust and the replacement Sixth Street Viaduct. Maltzan, an architect with a keen nose for new directions in culture and land use, came up with a brazen scheme: a quarter-mile-long, six-story high block of 438 apartments, built over shops and around a central concourse with restaurants, a grocery store, a bookshop, and public areas to hang out. It was like a skyscraper laid on its side, and it was conceived almost as a piece of infrastructure in anticipation of mass transit, with a connection to the First Street Bridge and a future Metro Red Line station.

One Santa Fe also incorporated plenty of shared

social amenities: a pool deck and hot tub, a fitness area, an outdoor barbecue with a view of the mountains. When it opened in 2011, the complex was a shock. Its scale was gigantic relative to surrounding buildings. It was a vivid red and white (since repainted by new owners in a strange orange and blue). The lifestyle it offered was a new one for L.A.: apartment dwellers were paying city-average rents to live alongside rail yards, a truck route, and industrial buildings, and above shops and restaurants. The air was poor and there was almost no green space anywhere nearby. But residents could gather in the outdoor rooms on the roof and terraces spread along its length. Nishanth Krishnamurthy took a studio apartment there during the pandemic. He works in community air protection for the South Coast AQMD, so he had an expert knowledge of the particulates swirling around him—but nonetheless he says he enjoyed living at One Santa Fe, adding that he was amazed by "its size and striking design" and its urban feel. "I love that when I look out my window or am out and about, I see actual people. Not just cars. Because of that, I feel like I'm part of a larger community and not like I'm going about it alone."

**Opposite: One Santa Fe is a community of apartments over shops and restaurants, at the scale of an urban village.**

One Santa Fe, 2021

Opposite: The lush roof of Treehouse Hollywood; above, a micro-bedroom.

There was also a radical mix of apartment sizes: studios and one-bedroom, two-bedroom, and three-bedroom apartments, with very large group living spaces. Twenty percent of the apartments were designated as affordable apartments. The owners rented those first and, according to Maltzan, by early morning on the day leasing began, "there was a line all the way down Santa Fe. If there was ever an indication of the need for affordable housing, that was it." The designers intended to mix up the demographics, to offer an alternative to the binary housing split in Los Angeles—apartments for the poor or young and old people without children, and houses for well-to-do families. The thinking was that a place like One Santa Fe could be home throughout adult life instead of the hopping around between dwelling types over life's phases that is commonplace in American life. "That's how you start to develop a real relationship to a neighborhood," says Maltzan, adding, "I thought we were making at the time a truly new form for Los Angeles in the way that people are used to

living here. It was a project that would have the ability, even through its scale, to create community through the types of spaces and mixed uses that existed there."

One Santa Fe was a new typology for Los Angeles—very large, mid-rise, mixed-use, mixed-demographic, mixed-income—and it was a bellwether of what was to come. Now this type of development can be found in South Park, Hollywood, Koreatown, and on major arterial streets. The projects get bigger and higher when they have density bonuses—permission to increase the Floor Area Ratio (FAR), which is real estate parlance for the number of units allowable on the site—the nearer they are to mass transit. However, in keeping with L.A.'s land use patterns and housing history, parking spaces are still mandatory, even close to transit because most Angelenos have not shifted to a car-free life, so now ever-taller luxury residential towers perch on ever-larger stacks of parking, known as parking podiums. Ambitious projects are coming to the Arts District, at a scale that will dwarf One Santa Fe. They involve global conglomerates and international architects but they stand on the shoulders of Maltzan's scheme, which projected the future, while incorporating the social elements of L.A.'s boutique and apartment-hotels.

## Treehouse and Co-Living

Michael Maltzan and the team that created One Santa Fe were not the only Angelenos thinking about new forms of community-centered living in the Southland. In late 2019, the property developer Prophet Walker and his investment partner Joe Green invited friends, journalists, and prospective tenants to a housewarming party in a new building in Hollywood called Treehouse. A large crowd of curious attendees roved around the blue-green five-story structure with roughened wood balconies. Exterior stairs and balconies led to the doorways of

Treehouse Hollywood's shared dining room.

eighteen suites of four or five bedrooms around shared dining and cooking areas. Each bedroom was petite (though each had its own bathroom). But there was an abundance of communal areas: a reception with a comfy sofa and a coffee bar, a laundry that doubles as an art room, a library with beaten leather chairs, a large cafeteria, and, the pièce de résistance, a rooftop terrace with garden chairs, bars, and vintage clawfoot bathtubs nestled in climbing vines, grasses, and ornamentals, as well as an olive tree, a California pepper tree, and a California live oak, all with a view of the Hollywood sign. This garden in the sky was designed by Sean Knibb, who had created the landscape at the Toy Factory. He had put these trees into immense pots and hoisted them up to the roof, where they are kept alive by a hidden superstructure that captures and recycles the water. "Nothing feels as good as being in a garden that feels wild and lush and rambling in a city that's very urban gridded and void of greenery," he says, as if he is describing a yard or a park and not a flat roof that's

five stories in the air. In his role as creative director for Treehouse (the architects were TheCaliforniaOffice), Knibb filled rooms with art and objects and furniture carefully chosen to look artfully unmatched. Knibb said he wanted to create the impression that the place was filled with mementos from different people's vacations. Walker said he was seeking something akin to the feeling he got in his grandparents' home, where "it was like you sat in a time capsule" surrounded by family history on the walls—degrees and pictures and *tchotchkes* past and present. This kind of undesign gave him the feeling of "being wrapped in a hug." That became their mantra with designing Treehouse and other buildings that would follow in an expansive rollout, says Walker: "Can we make our space feel like it's wrapped in a hug?"

Treehouse is a high-concept version of what's known as a co-living building. "Co-living" became a popular topic in L.A. around 2015 with the arrival of coworking, which in turn was a byproduct of the gig economy. Freelance workers could rent a desk in a

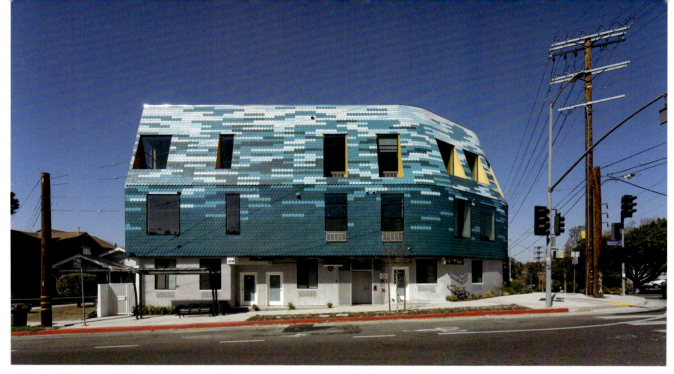

Monterey Apartments, also known as Arroyo, with colorful shingles, inspired by Victorian shingles in Heritage Park.

shared office and gain access to shared amenities like coffee and printers, along with some human company. The same logic was then applied to housing. Initially, developers shoehorned hives of tiny sleeping spaces (sometimes several beds in one room) into existing warehouses and large old houses, in neighborhoods including Venice, Koreatown, and Highland Park. It was a form of rental arbitrage, whereby investors would maximize the return on a building they leased or owned by subdividing it into multiple spaces for short-term lets at a higher per-square-foot price.

Rents were typically market rate. To anyone who wondered if this was hostel living by another name and at a higher cost, builders argued that the tiny personal space was offset by generous shared spaces and amenities that offered human connection in an atomized time. Co-living quickly became a new real estate product and companies like Common rolled them out at speed across Los Angeles and high-rent cities filled with young adults looking for a relatively

affordable home, plus instant friends. Some were characterful structures, like Monterey Apartments in Hermon, designed by Warren Techentin for 4-Site, with an unmissable scaly surface of sea-green and blue cement shingle tiles. They attract new arrivals and fledgling talents in creative industries who can live under the same roof and collaborate on projects, often using the facilities that are in the building itself. They mix the styling and amenities of boutique hotels with the hyper-sociability of a college dorm.

Treehouse was one of the first *ground-up* co-living buildings in Los Angeles, and it went further than the others in creating a distinct character and clear design for this new kind of communal living. For Walker and Green, it was both business and mission. The two men came from completely different life experiences. Green grew up in Santa Monica and went on to Harvard, where he became an investor in an early iteration of Facebook. "It's a sad thing about America, and in many ways, even more particularly about Los Angeles, that wealth buys you isolation," says Green. "We know that the farther people live apart, the longer they commute, the less happy they are." Walker is the child of a Black man whose family lived in the Watts area and a white woman who became addicted to heroin and "abandoned my sister and me in one of the drug houses at Nickerson Gardens," at the height of the crack epidemic in the early 1990s. While in prison, Walker created and participated in a two-year college degree program for inmates—for which he was later invited to join First Lady Michelle Obama as a guest at the 2015 State of the Union address—and on his release, studied engineering, moved into construction management, and then into real estate. He did well and started on the path Green had observed about America: "I was building stuff and I was making money and I got a place in Playa Vista, and I started truly feeling that wealth was buying me isolation." He says he yearned for something he had found during the tough times at Nickerson Gardens and then in prison. On Friday evenings, he recalls, "Everyone would go to their bars, and it would be an open mic. Some people would recite poetry. Some people would tell stories; some people would sing. The whole group would sing together. And that really got me thinking about how important it was to still have community and connection, even in the darkest of moments." Of course he did not want to recreate the harshness and soul-destroying character and management of these environments. But he also wanted a different approach from the big co-living builders who, in his view, were "all about density arbitrage, scale, scale, scale." Then he met Joe Green, "and he was really into building community and had worked on political campaigns. He was super deep into the psychedelic world. We're really different, but this is perfect. If multifamily housing, and having denser environments, is going to be the future, it should not be

such that that future is one where we're faceless. I want a depth of soul connection."

Walker and Green set their sights on creating Treehouse. The first residents moved into Treehouse Hollywood in late 2019. They had responded to a detailed application, with questions like "Please talk about a community cause that you're a part of" and "Tell us about a time when you helped a friend." The group of strangers got to know each other over meals in their suites and at dinners for the entire household held weekly. The first arrivals were able to choose their next co-residents. Jason E.C. Wright, a bibliophile and founder of the design research institute Burntsienna Research Society, was interviewed by tenants and made the cut, taking up residence in July 2020, in the middle of the pandemic. He says that following the collapse of a business and a relationship, Treehouse was a life-saver. After four years of a solitary life in Studio City, he was fascinated by the concept—which he understood as "a vertical village" or, as in *Star Trek*, "a land-based ship. So how do people engage in the spaces for extraversion, how do they work with spaces for introversion?" What does this mean to Americans, he wondered, whose "knowledge of communal living is dormitories on one end, cults on the other, and moving back home with your parents in the middle? I was curious about how that could work and what I could contribute to." Wright formed an extended "family" and thrived on the opportunities the space offered to launch communal activities, such as a show-and-tell art book club he created in the library. The pandemic put the project's very concept to the test. Tenants had to form COVID bubbles and eat in their rooms. A few people left, but most remained and stayed connected, watching out for each other or playing games together online from their rooms. Like Wright, some residents chose to move in during that time, to get away from isolation.

For Prophet Walker, who lived for several months in the building with his teenage daughter, this validated the Treehouse concept. "When you're in proximity and you know your neighbor, you can be supported by a neighbor."

At Treehouse the duo also hoped to accomplish something that Green said Americans are typically not very good at: "density and diversity." The group of forty or so residents has proved to be highly mixed in terms of race, though not of age. Residents tend to be young, though a few seniors have joined the throng. Many have sought out the intense level of companionship but still find that co-living is not always easy. A challenge, says Wright, is open communication within a large group that grew up within the same culture but often thinks very differently. "There is no default dean's office to go to, there's no complaint department. We're going to have to try to resolve this." People can overstep lines they did not know existed, and clear communication is an ongoing work in progress. But residents have run with the Treehouse concept and made it their own. They have iterated, like Wright's book events, or a gym that was set up by another tenant in the parking garage. It emerged that several residents were professional chefs, enriching the shared meals. Children living there are being raised by a village. On balance, reflects Wright, "this place has kind of restored my faith in humanity."

Treehouse Hollywood was only the start. In 2021, Walker and Green broke ground on a new building in Koreatown. This was a structure on a tight site, containing affordable studios, built in partnership with the charitable organization United Way. Meanwhile, they were busy taking their vision to Leimert Park. The

Prophet Walker (below) and Joe Green in the "treehouse" at Treehouse Hollywood.

team proposed an eight-story building on almost a half-acre by the Crenshaw/LAX Line's Leimert Park Station. It would have 101 apartments, a restaurant on the roof, and a market hall at ground level along with other businesses. The plan offers very few parking spaces—fifteen—saying that this makes sense for tomorrow's Angelenos, who will use the light rail. It would be a mix of co-living spaces and regular apartments with up to four bedrooms. Some would be set aside for low- and extremely low-income levels. Mainly, though, Walker wanted to create a bustling hub for people at all stages of life, as well as one that would attract neighbors, other people in Leimert Park. So it would be more than a "land-based ship"; it would be a social condenser for the area. In dreaming up ways to redesign living, Walker was continuing a Los Angeles tradition of building intentional community.

## Connected by Art: St. Elmo Village

Most Angelenos dwell in a spec-built house or apartment. Those with greater means can commission a custom-designed residence and put their personal stamp on it. A few seek a more intentional form of living, in a community that represents a belief system or a shared passion, often founded by a charismatic person like Walker at Treehouse. Sometimes these have taken the form of strange, even dangerous, cults or utopian colonies that rarely last long. But they can also be highly inspiring and endure as long as their founding ideal still binds people, as at St. Elmo Village and L.A. Eco-Village.

St. Elmo Village is one of those marvelous unexpected enclaves—a world within a world—that characterizes the gems of Los Angeles multifamily housing. It was created in 1969 by two Black artists, Rozzell Sykes and his nephew, Roderick Sykes, as a

The sign in front of St. Elmo Village signals the artfulness to come.

live-work haven for fellow creatives. It consists of ten cottages, a large studio, a six-unit apartment building, and a three-bedroom house on St. Elmo Drive in a mid-city neighborhood between La Brea Avenue and Venice and Washington Boulevards. Those are the basics. Driving there, the street is ordinary, populated with slightly rundown-looking apartment buildings and bungalows. On arriving mid-block, visitors see an explosion of bushes and trees in front of little wooden cottages with front porches, each painted a warm brown. A hand-painted sign for St. Elmo Village beckons visitors to a path, which is painted in a swirl of abstract shapes in acrylic red, yellow, orange, pink, grass green, and sky blue. The path leads to the back of the site, where it opens up into a wide driveway covered in the same brightly painted patterns. The driveway is bounded by the cottages, a circular outdoor seating area, an art studio, and, tucked in a back corner behind a gate, a pond. The whole ensemble is a visual paradise. There is not a lick of white paint in sight. All the buildings are painted "Village" colors, shades selected by Roderick Sykes: brown, blue, and green. Signs and sculptures are crafted from found bits of wood and metal; every corner of the place is touched by the human hand. Cacti, succulents, trees, and flowers abound.

When the Sykeses first moved in, this was a group of modest cottages that once served as stables for Mary Pickford's horses. They started showing their artwork at home and offering art classes to local kids. Then they learned that the site was going to be sold. With the help of then-Councilman Tom Bradley, as well as a lawyer friend and supporters of their artwork, they pulled together funds, bought the ten bungalows and garages, and created a nonprofit, dedicated to creating a "space of creativity." This would become a place where "children could create and learn, and adults could rediscover what they maybe forgot about," says Jacqueline Alexander-Sykes, an artist who is the widow of Roderick Sykes. The couple gave it a name: St. Elmo Village. It became a living canvas for their work and that of the neighborhood. They mounted public exhibitions and performances by numerous talents (including Merry Clayton and Lula Washington Dance Theatre). It became a hub for social activism, and serves as a polling place. "I like to say we elected Barack Obama, because the line was down the driveway," says Alexander-Sykes. St. Elmo Village is not a commune, nor is it collectively owned. "Most people who survived the '60s know that co-ops didn't work," says Alexander-Sykes matter-of-factly. "The intention is that everyone does their part. But the reality is that only two or three people out of twenty do everything." It is a nonprofit, with a board, formed in 1971. Residents rent units from the nonprofit corporation, administered by Alexander-Sykes, who handles most aspects of running the complex and also teaches classes. The rent covers access to the photography studio and art room, which are shared with non-residents who can come and pitch ideas for activities there. St. Elmo Village survived some tough times—especially during the 1980s, when drugs and

The art studio at St. Elmo Village.

The driveway and gathering space at St. Elmo Village is infused with the founders' artistic vision.

crack consumed the neighborhood—and now faces a new challenge: gentrification. Locals visit the Village for meetings about art, renters' rights, and social issues. After existing for more than five decades, St. Elmo Village is at a crossroads, following the death of its co-founder Roderick Sykes in 2021. Supporters and observers want to preserve and build on St. Elmo's role as a vital hub for primarily Black arts and activism. For Alexander-Sykes, who lives in a cottage surrounded by her beloved late husband's paintings and photographs, it is a monument to his vision. But she has building plans of her own: to realize Sykes's dream to turn one of their properties they own into artist studios and dwellings. St. Elmo Village attests to the power of an individual to create a place that transcends home, becoming an institution in the neighborhood. One of St. Elmo Village's many community projects is produce distribution. "The surrounding area supports us—it's a mutual support system," reflects Alexander-Sykes. "If it weren't for the community being part of us, we wouldn't have existed for this long. There's a sense of being part of something bigger than themselves."

## L.A. Eco-Village

St. Elmo Village and its management chose to remain a rental community, albeit one connected by shared values. Some groups believe cooperative ownership is integral to the vision, as expressed at Los Angeles Eco-Village, an intentional community that aims to model sustainability in its broadest sense.

If you head north on Vermont Avenue toward the 101 freeway, as you approach First Street, you pass a supermarket, a vape business, a Kentucky Fried Chicken, and a Little Caesars Pizza—in sum, a regular Los Angeles strip. Turn right on First, however, and then right again, and you'll find yourself on Bimini

Place, and here things just feel different. There are chalk drawings on the road and the sidewalk; a yard in front of a large old building with a tile roof and arched doorway and windows contains a community garden, filled with trees and vegetables, odd artworks (a parrot on a welcome sign, a Buddha's head in a plant pot), and a case filled with books free to passersby, atop a lime-green stand. Beside this is a driveway leading to a light industrial space, which has become a hangout with potted plants, chairs in a circle under a tree, and a wooden hut with a sign in front that reads, in English and Spanish: "Los Angeles Ecovillage Institute: reinventing how we live in the city for a higher quality of life at a lower environmental impact." It advertises events, educational tours, a learning garden, and workshops.

L.A. Eco-Village is a community of about fifty households who live as intentional neighbors in three large buildings in this neighborhood in north Koreatown. The main building is a Spanish-style building dating back a century, that surrounds a large central court filled with vegetable patches, a chicken run, an outdoor kitchen and dining area, a laundry area with a washing machine hooked up to a gray-water system, and rainwater cisterns that irrigate some of the fruit trees. Within the complex are smaller courts; one is by a shady feijoa tree and nearby converted garages, now converted into workshops for making art or furniture in the toolshed. The lobby of the building, another group social space, displays a row of paintings devoted to icons of social justice movements. The entire place feels handmade and uncoiffed, because the building and its systems are all recycled and repurposed. Ian McIlvaine, founding board member and an

Opposite: Entrance to L.A. Eco-Village on Bimini Place

architect, notes that the courtyard arrangement was a great foundation: "The Eco-Village community was able to flourish here."

This place is many things—a home, a place of political activism and community-building, and a model of permaculture and energy efficiency dating back to before those terms entered common parlance. It is also, significantly, a limited-equity housing cooperative whose buildings sit on land owned by a Community Land Trust (CLT), one of only a handful in California. Some residents are owner-members in the co-op and some are renter-members. The co-op has a ninety-nine-year ground lease with the CLT and pays it a monthly rent, keeping housing costs for its members substantially lower than local market-rate rents.

Eco-Village is a collective venture, but it was driven by a woman with formidable energy and a commitment to an idea and to the complicated organizing to achieve it: Lois Arkin. Arkin was on track for a conventional Los Angeles lifestyle. In 1961, she and her then husband, both employed in the aerospace industry, bought a house in Chatsworth for $23,000. Then she started studying anthropology and found herself fascinated by one of the spiritual communities that had set up in the Santa Susana Mountains. Her research into collective ownership radicalized her thinking about how to live sustainably, in a way that included but went beyond living more lightly on the land. It had to do with housing affordability. "An essential component of sustainability is that you have to own land and buildings in order to keep housing and land affordable to future generations that have incomes similar to the people who occupied the land and buildings when you began your project," Arkin says. So she threw herself into the cohousing movement. In 1980, she created the nonprofit CRSP (Cooperative Resources and Services Project) Institute for Urban Ecovillages. In 1993, she co-founded

L.A. Eco-Village brings earthiness and intentional community into a highly urban part of Los Angeles.

the Los Angeles Eco-Village as a project of CRSP. The idea was for a cooperative housing community that would model green technologies like solar power and recycled water and waste, and transmit these values throughout the neighborhood. The group initially leased space in two buildings at the north end of Koreatown, and they pieced together a complex deal to finance and buy these and one other property. With the support of a board, L.A. Eco-Village has evolved over the years into a case study for eco-design, co-living, and co-ownership. Its impact has gone far beyond its building. "Some of the things I am very proud of are the number of city transforming projects," says McIlvaine, referencing various initiatives that supported bike culture in the Southland, including L.A. Bicycle Kitchen, a bike repair co-op, and the L.A. County Bicycle Coalition, which fights for bike lanes and other safety measures.

The journey was not always easy. In fact, Arkin cites Diana Leafe Christian, a guru within the ecovillage movement, who says, "The longest, hardest personal growth experience you will ever have is living in an intentional community." Not everyone shoulders the load. There were even times when members seemed to be fundamentally out of sync with the basic mission of the community, says Arkin, such as those who did not believe natural cross-ventilation kept their dwellings cool enough. "It just didn't occur to me that someone who wanted to live in an ecovillage would want to have air conditioning, so we never created a policy against it." After some early years that were fraught with infighting, the Village sought help from experts in conflict resolution. Now they secure new residents through a long process of community approvals. It's a process that seems arduous to some, says McIlvaine, "but this is not just a negotiation about a commodity [housing)]. Rather, it is about building a community, so it necessarily takes time."

The Community Land Trust seems like a great solution in principle, but in practice it turns out this too is complicated. First, it involves a great deal of work. "[A CLT is] so difficult because there is a requirement for community representation and committee decision-making," says Helen Leung, who has worked on housing issues on both a local city and federal level. "It can take a couple of years to figure out the rules—who are they serving? Who is the community? There are endless meetings to create the structure where you cap the equity that any single person who's there can earn." Moreover, the very thing that stabilizes the land value is the thing that works against them being popular. Arkin's fundamental issue is with speculation in land and uncontrollable jumps in price. Yet that is exactly what attracts people to buy property in Los Angeles. The land appreciates every ten years in California, not the building that sits on it. McIlvaine says, "We specifically allowed for appreciation of a member's equity in honor of that principle," but the amount is symbolic, not a financial incentive. Nonetheless, there is a growing CLT movement in Los Angeles, which was boosted in 2021 when county supervisors authorized funding for the development of five pilot CLTs, each in a supervisorial district.

In 2020, Arkin, by then in her eighties and holed up due to the pandemic, penned a reflective blog post entitled, "The Ups and Downs of Reinventing How We Live in Cities." It was illustrated with a photo of a group of people mixed in race and age, in a circle by a sign advertising "Free Music Lessons." Arkin meditated on growing older and looked back at the endless bureaucratic hurdles she had surmounted on the road to achieving an ecovillage. She offered a to-do list for its next stage, including: urban teaching farm, geothermal energy, neighborhood solar, research center for remediation of toxic soils, car-free streets in our two-block neighborhood, biological living machine for gray and black water, etc. And she told readers where she wanted to be buried—directly in the earth at the courtyard garden, with the worms, no coffin. However, she was not planning on dying anytime soon. With living to 100 in her sights, she wrote, "I have started an 'old women's group' of local environmental activists which now meets monthly online. I find I am not alone as I age, and that collectively we have so much to offer, but then again, for most younger folks, 'everything's online.' And I find that more and more of those young people seek advice and resources from [Los Angeles Ecovillage Institute], whether for their academic research or a place to live where people know your name and don't think you're weird if you compost and ride a bike, and/or because they want to start intentional communities, cohousing, ecovillages. It has been exhilarating to see the awareness and desire for community grow."

# 09

# BACK TO THE BUNGALOW COURT
## ADUs and the New Low-Rise Housing

All the exciting creativity in multifamily dwelling design does not alter the harsh reality of housing in L.A. in the 2020s, which is that it is extremely expensive and largely available to the rich, those prepared to live with multiple roommates, and some of the poor. People in the middle are squeezed. The workforce—those who form the backbone of the community like teachers or nurses—find in many L.A. neighborhoods that they earn not nearly enough to afford market-rate rents or home ownership and just too much to be eligible for "affordable" housing. So middle-income people move further and further from pricey city centers, and then spend hours commuting, clogging the roads with traffic and pollution. It is an untenable way for a region to function. Yet there is widespread voter resistance to kissing goodbye to the garden city and simply allowing greater density in all residential neighborhoods. So planners and policymakers have tried to come up with neat solutions that maintain the existing urban fabric through adding additional units

**Opposite: Peach Pit, an 800-square-foot ADU**

in the backyards of single-family homes. State laws that took effect in the late 2010s and 2020s, authorizing the construction of between one and ten dwellings on lots in R1 zones, heralded the revival of the low-scale multifamily complex, along with new opportunities for extended family living and aging in place.

## Accessory Dwelling Units and Extended Family Living

By the time the new millennium rolled around, more than seventy percent of residential neighborhoods in the city of Los Angeles were zoned for single-family houses only. This included neighborhoods that contained low-rise multifamily buildings like bungalow courts and two-, three-, and four-plexes dating back to early last century that were later down-zoned. Meanwhile, the population had boomed, from around four million in Los Angeles County in 1950 to over nine million in 2000; and from just under two million to almost four million in the City of L.A., making it home to more residents than you would find within most U.S. states. The housing squeeze was also happening across

other rapidly growing, booming California cities, so policymakers concurred that the state needed to build around some three million more homes, with 800,000 of them in L.A. County, around 450,000 in the City of Los Angeles, spread across different income levels. These numbers irritated many homeowning Angelenos, because building more homes means more large, multistory apartments and more congestion, and a limit on the lifestyle synonymous with L.A. for so long: the house and yard with plenty of parking in a pleasant garden city.

So some urban designers and planners pondered whether it was possible to achieve both: keep the beloved low-rise lifestyle and add more housing. One of them was Dana Cuff, head of UCLA's think tank cityLAB. Cuff had grown up in Orange County when it was still filled with orange groves. She knew the housing status quo did not work, but she strongly believed that Los Angeles had to grow its supply of homes in a way "that's really in keeping with the suburban fabric." She saw an opportunity in a type of secondary home that already existed widely: the granny flat or "accessory dwelling unit" (known as an ADU) in the backyard of a single-family home. There were already thousands of them, built illegally in converted garages or as backyard "studios." If only these could be multiplied, Los Angeles could realize 100,000 units of new housing "with just twenty percent of L.A.'s half-million single-family lots," said Cuff. She spent ten years working with her cityLAB students to figure out how to turn this into policy. In 2015, she invited media to come visit the BIHOME, a small pavilion at UCLA made of pipe frame shrink-wrapped in plastic like oversized bubble wrap, with nooks and crannies

City-sponsored Pilot ADU in Highland Park designed by Office of: Office, Elizabeth Timme/LA-Más

to let lizards, birds, and other wildlife forage and nest. The 350-square-foot structure was a fanciful demonstration house with an ecological overlay; it was meant to model the idea of a lightweight, easy-to-build backyard dwelling that could be multiplied many times over without putting pressure on a single-family neighborhood. The designer of the structure, Kevin Daly, architect of Tahiti Housing for Community Corp and several other exemplary multifamily complexes, and also Cuff's spouse, called this approach "distributed density." Meanwhile, in Hancock Park, a man named Ira Belgrade had built an unpermitted small dwelling in his backyard. Code enforcers came after him, and he wound up in a lengthy and public dispute. It caught the media's attention, so he took advantage of the platform to spread his message. "There are approximately something like 50,000 unpermitted units in Los Angeles alone," Belgrade told the local CBS-News affiliate. "People need these units, whether it's to rent out or for personal use. We need them now. We need the

housing." Belgrade and Cuff became part of a growing movement to legalize ADUs. Cuff and longtime city planner Jane Blumenfeld joined forces with Santa Monica–based assemblymember Richard Bloom, and together they authored state Assembly Bill 2299, which became law in 2017. Several more related bills followed, including one that added JADUs, or Junior ADUs, an extra dwelling of up to 500 square feet that could be built within the shell of a proposed or existing single-family residence. In 2020, AB 68 took effect, expanding the options for the location and form of ADUs and preventing local governments from adopting ordinances that would thwart the construction of ADUs.

Despite resistance from some homeowner organizations, it turned out that a lot of Angelenos liked the ADU idea. Records show that 11,500 of them were permitted in the city of L.A. between 2017 and 2019. They were a means to add square footage to a home without disruptive construction on an existing house. Besides, setback requirements were eased and—in a

The Midnight Room ADU opens onto the shared spaces of the extended living space.

Interior of the Leong-Alvarado ADU in Atwater Village

dramatic break from the past rules for new dwellings—an ADU did not require an extra parking space. They were a vehicle to pay the mortgage on a costly home, through renting out. As building contractor Diahanne Payne, founder of Illegal Additions Made Legal, put it succinctly: "Your house can have a baby. You can make the baby work." People built them for all sorts of other uses: for work (an office), for respite (a meditation or yoga studio), as a guest house, and for extended family. These petite houses became a venue for experimentation among young design firms that produced a wide range of designs playing with form and pushing new design and delivery systems.

The advent of ADUs turned thousands of Angelenos into landlords with a small onsite income property. On the one hand this harkened back to lot-packing—a practice identified by the scholar of low-income housing, Paul Groth. On the other it represented a break from what had later become the solitary mode of living of many American households.

"The ADU is a typology that is questioning the way that we live together and share space," observes Melissa Shin, who has designed several delightful backyard residences in collaboration with her sister Amanda and their firm, Shin Shin. "It's a very strange idea, actually, to most people that you would share your private property with a stranger." What this means for designers like Shin is figuring out how to enable people to coexist in a way that was not mutually invasive. "It's a lot about finding that balance between a private space, but also understanding that you're living as part of a community." Shin Shin designed an ADU called the Peach Pit—with a distinctive façade with an off-center curving archway and careful arrangement of inside-outside living spaces—that garnered a lot of press. It was built for Amanda Shin. "When we wanted to do a project for ourselves, the only house that we could afford came with so many problems that made the project nearly infeasible," recalls Melissa Shin. She explains that "part of our model for financing it was

Prefabricated ADU in Brentwood by Cover, with two bedrooms and a bathroom in 910 square feet.

the rental unit." Unusually, they put the ADU at the front of the lot and then arranged the structures so they faced away from each other. The main house has a large balcony that faces towards the back, while the front of the ADU faces the street.

Conversely, some ADUs are designed to engage with the main house in a more direct way, because the goal is connection. The cost of land, coupled with other high costs of living, such as childcare, has caused families to co-invest in extended-family compounds made of a house and an ADU. This can provide just enough distance for nuclear family-style independence, and enough closeness to enable adults to care for senior parents, or for grandparents to tend the children of their children. Together, they can spread the costs. The common ground is both physical and financial. The architects, Rebecca Rudolph and Catherine Johnson of Design, Bitches, turned the back of an Atwater Village bungalow into The Midnight Room, a small dwelling to house the visiting parents of their clients,

Pastor Alvarado and Gennifer Leong-Alvarado. They created a simple but elegant shed-like structure, made of exposed marine-grade plywood walls and Douglas fir beams, with deep sea-green tiling, and navy blue cement-board siding. Between the house and the baby house are shared spaces—a fire pit, a pool, a covered veranda—arranged as a series of outdoor rooms. "We wanted to give them a sense of privacy while being connected to their family," Johnson told the *Los Angeles Times*. "The families can peek across the yard and see if they are eating outside, but it also allows them some visual privacy. There is clear space for mobility. We wanted to make it flexible for them, easy for them to get around, but still feel like a beautiful, wonderful, independent-feeling space. It's nice to connect generations rather than isolate families."

For some families, the complex is a permanent home. Chet Callahan was commissioned by a couple with two teenage children who wanted the grandparents from San Diego to join them. Real estate in their neighborhood in Culver City was so pricey on their middle-class income they decided to try and cram everyone onto the same site. At early meetings, says Callahan, the clients mostly talked about basic programmatic needs: bedrooms, baths, and so on. But he urged them to think more about the kind of closeness and distance they wanted with each other. In such a confined space, they needed to get the connectivity right and create a mix of communal spaces—some for the four, some for all six—along with private space for each individual. Out of many meetings came a solution that involved adding a shared eating area onto the back of the original house, forming a meeting point between the residences.

One thing ADUs could not fully solve was the affordability challenge. As ADUs were on the brink of becoming legal, the designer-policymakers Elizabeth Timme/LA-Más, the Bloomberg Innovation Team and the Mayor's Office at the City of L.A. invited a homeowner to volunteer to build one, with support from financiers Genesis L.A. Trent Wolbe and Grace Lee stepped up and, in 2019, unveiled their new two-story backyard home in Highland Park. It was impressive, a witty spin on the craftsman architecture of the area, with sky-blue siding and an open kitchen-dining-living area with picture rails, warm woods, and honey linoleum floors. It was large for an ADU, at almost 1400 square feet including a garage. But "it was expensive, it was time-consuming, and it was really complicated," said Wolbe at the opening. The costs and complications included building on a hilly site and dealing with numerous entities including a host of contractors and the local HPOZ, or Historic Preservation Overlay Zone, whose design edits caused cost overruns in the thousands. "This was an experiment to see—what red tape do we run into? How can we get financing? How do people manage design?" said Mayor Eric Garcetti

at the ribbon-cutting. Wolbe and Lee moved into their pilot ADU with their daughter and cats, where they now "live happily," and rented out the main house. Out of this process came a loosening of some rules, like strict design controls by HPOZs, and it also led to a rise in interest in offsite construction, using prefabricated modules as a means of speeding up the process.

Multiple firms have emerged, promising to streamline costs thanks to optimization by artificial intelligence. Cover, a Gardena-based company, employs as many tech engineers as architects, and they sell prefabricated backyard structures that deploy computational design and software to make house-buying more akin to ordering a car. Buyers go online to pick and choose the elements of the ADU, which are then mostly fabricated in a factory. One of Cover's funders was also an early investor in AirBnB and SnapChat. "We take care of the entire process, from the design stage to the engineering, permitting, manufacturing, delivery, and installation," says company CEO Alexis Rivas. "We're the single point of contact for the client." Clients included a Brentwood family that commissioned a 900-square-foot, two-bedroom backyard house, complete with a full kitchen and an island in the open living-kitchen-dining area, for the mother/grandmother who was downsizing from her primary home in Palm Springs and wanted to be closer to family as she aged. The steel structure, finished in pale fiber cement panels, went up speedily—forty-five days in 2021, says Rivas. That was after the preparation of a site and building a foundation, trenching a sewer line, and then connecting to utilities—a water line and gas or electric. After all those costs, even robot-assisted ADUs can cost around $350,000 to $400,000.

ADUs have largely filled "a niche in housing for young professionals who can't quite afford to buy a home, but want to rent something nice with a yard and the charm of a single-family residence," notes Shin. Yet they do play a much-needed role in relieving some pressure on constantly increasing housing prices, observes Frederick Zimmerman, professor of public health and urban planning at UCLA. "Newly constructed—and thoughtfully designed—ADUs may not prove to be an affordable solution for low-income Angelenos. Yet they are an important part of the ways in which housing supply can rise to meet housing demand and keep prices lower than they otherwise would be." They have also provided the means for families and other groups who might want to co-exist in formerly single-family neighborhoods to do so. Moreover, they have challenged Angelenos' assumptions about size and household make-up of home. "I think that everyone is rethinking how they inhabit space, how much space they need," reflects Shin, adding, "I feel like I am representing a generation of people who actually do embrace this communal aspect of living together more. Not that people hadn't before, but we're going back to that."

## New Rules for Single-Family Neighborhoods

The ADU solved some problems, but it primarily benefited homeowners and perpetuated the asymmetric landlord-renter relationship. This was fine for people comfortable with renting, but not for those who also wanted to be homeowners, especially those who had been kept off of the property ladder for so long—people of color. Two new laws—Senate Bills 9 and 10, passed in 2021—increased the numbers of dwellings allowable on a single-family lot along with the right to split a lot in half (lot split), and thereby expanded in one stroke the pool of home sites in the state of California. Meanwhile, the City of Los Angeles launched a challenge to designers to explore how these new laws could birth a new generation of fourplexes and small apartment buildings centered on connected space that might also open up new opportunities for owning a home.

In 2021, an architect named Michael Anderson published a book called *Urban Magic: Vibrant Black*

**Green Alley Housing** proposes live-work duplexes opening onto a pedestrianized alley.

and *Brown Communities Are Possible*. He wrote about his decades-long efforts to help regenerate Black neighborhoods in South L.A. For him, there was an essential tool to create urban magic: homeownership for Black families rather than renting apartments, however lovely they might be. For those denied access to home ownership through zoning and redlining and racially restrictive covenants, apartment-living has long been bound up with exclusion from economic benefits. "White families have around twelve times the wealth of African American families and ten times the wealth of Hispanic families," reported Danielle Kurtzleben in a 2015 Vox exploration of America's "yawning racial wealth gap." This gap was in large part due to the disparity in owner-occupied real estate which, as of 2010, accounted for forty-two percent of the median homeowner's wealth, per the National Association of Home Builders. So homeownership would put households on a firmer foundation and, says Anderson, generate more property tax revenues, which would improve the infrastructure and the schools in those neighborhoods. Even though he had developed a row of single houses on Vernon Avenue in the Leimert Park neighborhood, he believed the answer lay not so much in single-family home ownership but rather in co-owned, intergenerational complexes, like the one in St. Louis that he grew up in, where "my great-grandfather actually built a fourplex house, and we lived in one unit with my father and mother; my great aunt and her son lived in another unit. My father's mother and father lived in another unit. And then we had another family member living in yet another unit. And it was actually a nice way to see the family every day and play in the backyard together. It was a beautiful relationship

Opposite: Hidden Gardens proposed four two-story dwellings interwoven with gardens.

at that time." For several years he has been working on a strategy to get federal support for Black families, putting in equity so they can purchase a triplex or fourplex and live in one dwelling while renting out the others to their family members or other tenants—akin to the FHA support of mortgages for private homes for primarily white people back in the mid twentieth-century. He wanted many other children to experience what he had, thanks to his great-grandfather. "I was only five or six years old, but I felt so proud when we turned the corner and there's our house."

Anderson was not alone in thinking about this kind of model. Observing the success of ADUs, policymakers and planners pushed for an expansion of allowable backyard dwellings and in 2021 Senate Bills 9 and 10 were signed into law allowing more dwellings as well as lot splitting in R1 zones. Proponents argued that this subdividing of a lot presented the opportunity for expanding homeownership, which could help right old wrongs. "The racial-justice reckoning of the last two years has made clear that we need to grapple with all of the ways we have excluded homeowners of color, particularly from the L.A. version of the American dream," said Christopher Hawthorne, the city's chief design officer, appointed by Mayor Eric Garcetti. He was speaking just after the murder of George Floyd at the hands of police in Minneapolis on May 25, 2020, which turbo-charged a conversation already bubbling up among planners and policymakers about the structural racism built into housing in America.

## The Low-Rise Housing Challenge

In 2020, in anticipation of the passage of the new laws, Hawthorne and a team at the City of Los Angeles sponsored a design challenge, entitled Low-Rise: Housing Ideas for Los Angeles. The goal was to make an aesthetic case for this increase in density—"gentle density," as planners have called it, or the "missing middle," between a house and a mid- or high-rise apartment building—along with the benefits in equity and community life that could result, all at a scale that neighbors could live with. Gentle density already had a model: the low-rise housing of the last century, "going back to bungalow courts, garden apartments, early modernist experiments, which remains a lot of the most desirable housing in Los Angeles," says Hawthorne. In a sense this was going back to the future. The new laws offered an opportunity to restore many neighborhoods to the mix of low-rise houses and multifamily units that were the norm until they were dramatically downzoned—by sixty percent in the 1970s, according to Greg Morrow, a professor of real estate development and design—pushing apartments to the peripheries of R1 zones and causing a squeeze on houses (raising housing costs across the entire state, according to the California Legislative Analyst's Office) and perpetuating racial segregation.

These arguments for expanding the dwellings allowable on a lot and lot splitting did not persuade everyone. Many homeowner and resident groups in neighborhoods from Leimert Park to Hancock Park, from L.A. County to Marin County, put up a furious battle against Senate Bills 9 and 10. Some wanted no change to single-family zoning. Others feared displacement, saying the propositions would spawn a land grab by greedy speculative developers who would demolish older, stabilized rental buildings. Several affordable housing developers in Los Angeles refused to support the bills.

Low-Rise: Housing Ideas for Los Angeles took the optimistic view. Several hundred designers from all over the world participated and when the submissions came in, many proposed flexible dwellings that could accommodate different-sized households or a mix of generations, in architectural designs that were a contemporary variant on courtyard living. The winning proposal in the subdivision category, for example, reactivates alley spaces in Northeast L.A. with Green Alley Housing, a concept for a network of live-work duplexes from Louisa Van Leer Architecture and a team. The first-place winners in the fourplex category, Omgivning and Studio MLA, imagined four units wrapped around a shared outdoor space in the middle of the parcel. In place of the front lawn, Omgivning's team proposed giving that space to the community to be planted with shade trees which, if replicated along the street, would build a linear network of new, public green space. Frogtown Four, by Bestor Architecture and a team, took second place; the designers proposed fourplexes of vertical bungalows with shared open space, recessed into the landscape to reduce their height and maintain the low urban fabric.

Projects emphasized community engagement, rewilded landscapes, opportunities for market gardens, more walkable living, as well as smart orientation for passive cooling, along with solar, gray water, and all-electric appliances. "Many of the compelling proposals were really smart about sustainability and energy use," said Hawthorne, adding that this connects to "questions of shared space and learning to live in a little bit less interior space, and maybe figuring out how to design our outdoor space so we can take advantage of the climate here." There was another dimension to the proposals: the organizers had asked design teams to think not only about the physical design of buildings, but also creative ownership models. Teams proposed various new cooperative housing models, particularly community land trusts. They offered up an image of living that was centered on shared space but also went beyond regular property owner-renter arrangements and modeled various alternatives to traditional home ownership. "We think by opening up this territory to new housing options there are multiple paths to affordability and homeownership that are possible within that," said Hawthorne. "It's really important to think about how it connects to homeownership."

The Low-Rise challenge produced extremely thoughtful designs that garnered attention from designers and planners. The concepts were not necessarily applicable, due to existing codes—on minimum setbacks, passageways, sizes of rear and front yards, and, of course, parking—and cost of land in the 2020s versus the 1920s, which is so high in so many neighborhoods that builders would likely maximize the square footage and rent or sell at market rate, not give it over to lovely linear parks. Still, it expanded the understanding of what home in Los Angeles could be.

**Tall bungalows stand behind the existing house in the Frogtown Four design proposal.**

# 10

# ENLIGHTENED LANDLORDS

The reality is that to live in a multifamily building—even the most charming of them—is, for most people, to be a renter, and to be a renter is to be on the wrong end of a power and equity imbalance. "We want a world without rent," says Anthony Carfello, a writer and curator who fights for renters rights as a member of the L.A. Tenants Union. "We want to envision new systems." Absent new systems, renters can at best hope to land in a municipality with reasonable rent protections and in buildings with good landlords. While stories of bad landlords are legion—and undeniably, property owners can match those with stories of bad renters—there are those who take their responsibilities as "housing providers" seriously. Some go further and try to tweak the system with hopes of recalibrating the balance of power, and even creating a sense of community.

**Opposite: View from a staircase at Spicy Watermelon**

## The Neighborhood Investment Company (Nico)

In the early decades of housing development in Los Angeles, a good number of landlords were small builders, mom-and-pop enterprises that might only own a few apartment buildings or just one, perhaps a duplex or fourplex that they themselves lived in, along with their renters. Since the 1970s, a growing number of residential buildings have been scooped up or built by faceless investment bankers, Wall Street firms, and real estate investment trusts (REITs). Many of them are headquartered outside Los Angeles and have little concern about the local impacts of their acquisitions. Some do. One is the Neighborhood Investment Company (Nico), which has tested a dual strategy aimed at empowering the tenants both financially and in terms of connection to place.

Spicy Watermelon is a marvelous bungalow court at 1412 Echo Park Avenue, built in the early 1930s by a developer named George L. McCallister who initially blasted the name "McCallister Manor" in a neon sign on the roof. His architect, Nathan Black, created eight two-story buildings, containing thirty-two units in total, that step down the hillside from Fairbanks Place to Echo Park Avenue. It has a narrow central alley which is bisected by passageways and leads to an open court. It has also been known simply as Echo Park Court and, later, "Big Mama" in honor of a beloved building manager. Around sixty people of all ages and backgrounds live in this complex, which feels like more than courtyard housing; its "streets" and winding narrow pathways make it feel as if an entire section of an old town on the Mediterranean has been lifted and plunked down on the hills of L.A. While walking around in early 2021 with a resident, Nicholas Shuminsky, a neighbor stuck her head out of the window to chat. At any moment you expected people to leap out of doorways and start dancing. At that point they had reason to be cheerful about their home. Over the decades, the complex had become rundown, devoid of greenery, and its exterior had settled into a dirty cream appearance. New owners, named Timberlane, purchased the property in the early 2010s and painted the entire place magenta, inspiring the nickname "Spicy Watermelon." Sizzling as this was, it was an investment and branding strategy. "The goal is for this to look like a Moroccan boutique hotel," said Timberlane's John Chaffetz, according to a *Bloomberg* article in 2015. "This strategy is straight out of the developer playbook," wrote the reporter Ben Steverman. "Buy neglected apartment buildings in promising neighborhoods, renovate, raise rents, and fill them with young professionals." This strategy was also potentially destructive to existing residents of Echo Park, an old neighborhood filled with low-income workers, many of them Latino, whose rents were rising in tandem with the supply of barista-made coffee and smashed avocado toast. So Chaffetz changed lanes, partnered up with a young developer named Max Levine, and

together they formed Nico Echo Park. This REIT had a difference. It was a certified B Corporation, meaning "it is deemed to be as committed to its social mission—to preserve rent-controlled apartments and give longtime residents more say in how their neighborhoods grow and change," explained Jenna Chandler in *Curbed Los Angeles*. The concept was that everyone in Echo Park should benefit—at least somewhat—from the gentrification of the neighborhood caused in part by developers like Timberlane. Nico Echo Park offered the public $10 shares in their portfolio—Spicy Watermelon and two other properties—with different redemption rights offered for investors from Echo Park. They offered residents of their eighty apartments a "Community Wealth Grant" of $1,000. This REIT "was a promising concept," said Shuminsky, "with potential to bridge the equity gap between renters and owners during a time when home ownership is out of reach for most Angelenos." Nico Echo Park also tackled another negative of renting: lack of agency over one's domain. They brought in a landscape design firm, Terremoto, and polled tenants at Spicy Watermelon about what plants they wanted. The resulting greenery, setting off the pink, is glorious. They planted jacaranda trees and native plants along with, in the words of Terremoto founder David Godshall, "a planting palette that speaks to this slightly old Hollywood, romantic, cinematic history of the city." They also created a vegetable garden in the back court and encouraged residents to grow and eat the produce, and to use the space as a social hangout. "In this culture, renting was really stigmatized because homeownership is almost fetishized," says Levine. "To us, the real magic really has to do with how the residents have made the space their own."

Nico Echo Park was launched during the pandemic and became a short-lived experiment. To fulfill the

New landscaping and fresh paint revitalize the vintage bungalow court.

mandate as a benefit corporation, they spent capital on subsidizing rent for tenants who lost income during the COVID-19 quarantine. They were not able to attract enough small investors during that time and, by the end of 2021, they closed Nico, giving back the capital plus a return of 5.4 percent. Spicy Watermelon and the other two buildings in their Echo Park portfolio were put up for sale. This meant that while tenants would hold on to stabilized rents, per L.A. law, new owners would have no obligation to maintain the hot-pink color or the vegetable garden, nor to find ways to make the renters feel less like renters. It was a discussion about the massive gulf between homeowners and renters that led to the founding of Nico. "The genesis

of the idea was, housing is broken," says Frank Melli, vice president of operations for the company. "There's renting, and on the other side is homeownership, which has become extremely inaccessible for a vast majority of the population. So is there a product in the middle that bridges that?" They could not figure out a "product" that would bridge that gap, and landed instead on the Neighborhood REIT, whose goals they continue to advance, though Nico now consults for other property owners. Helen Leung, who has worked on housing issues at the City of Los Angeles and the Obama White House, was on Nico Echo Park's board. She points out that their strategy was very unlikely to produce equity gains similar to that of home ownership or even a

Spicy Watermelon façade on Echo Park Avenue.

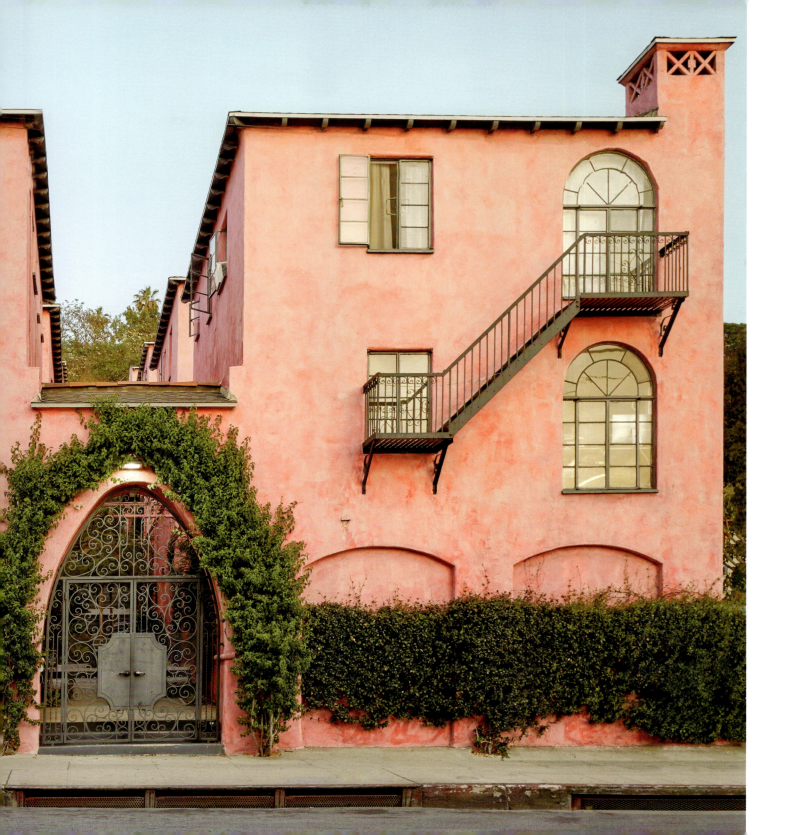

regular REIT. However, she admired Nico Echo Park, saying, "It was a successful and inspiring initial test of a new type of intervention with community ownership, housing stability, and community wealth building." She especially admired "its commitment to sustainability by buying existing assets, and honoring the tenants who are there." As for Levine, he is using the tools of the industry—real estate—to try and soften its inequities. "Rental housing," he says, "is a bad product and people know that tolerance for bad products—where you exploit people as a standard part of your business—in an era of social media and enhanced activism and housing as a human right just doesn't work anymore."

## The Third Street Compound

The tenants' experience at Spicy Watermelon reveals a truth about multifamily—rental—living in Los Angeles, which is that, for good and ill, residents' well-being can change on a dime. Take Bowen Court in Pasadena, for example, the bungalow court that started this narrative. As of this writing, it is owned by a man named Kostas Fergadis. He bought it in 1975 because he loved it and, until recently, he would come and sit in the office on the second level of the one-time teahouse and simply watch the goings-on in the pastoral court below. "Brokers want to buy it, and I say it's not for sale—the biggest bungalow court in Pasadena!" exclaims Fergadis with pride. When ownership eventually changes, the charmed lives of his tenants may also change. Fergadis is not the only property owner in Los Angeles making life pleasant for his tenants. There are a good many one could cite, but to this author one stands out, in the neighborhood of Ocean Park, a few blocks from the Gehry-built apartments. Tomas Fuller and William

**Tomas Fuller, left, and William Kelly in their Edenic compound.**

Kelly are a couple who bought a piece of land on Third Street in the 1990s, when the neighborhood was very run-down. They built themselves a new house on that site. When two sites next door came up for sale, each with rental bungalows on them, they bought those, too. Then they hired one of L.A.'s best landscape designers, Jay Griffith, to knit the three sites together with a garden. After that they invited a protégé of Griffith's, Sean Knibb, designer at Treehouse and the Toy Factory, to further develop this complex, adding more plants, creating pathways and nooks, private seating areas, a barbeque pit, and a croquet lawn. They invited all the tenants, some of whom are paying below-average rents, to make the most of the garden. Then they asked Knibb to add giant succulents and palms to the sidewalk, too, so the landscaping extends into the street for all passersby to enjoy. Singles, couples, and families with children live and hang out together at this lush Xanadu, presided over by Fuller and Kelly. They have nicknamed their little idyll "Tales of the City South," after Armistead Maupin's famed *Tales of the City* novels and TV adaptation about a house full of unconventional characters living under the stern and loving command of their landlady, Anna Madrigal. Residents also call the Fuller-Kelly estate, affectionately, the "Third Street compound." As Fuller and Kelly see it, there is a financial return for them: they get stability instead of the costs that come with constant turnover of tenants. Beyond that, they get company. They had originally looked at buying a house in a fancy part of the Westside. But, says Kelly, "if I lived in a house that's up in Bel Air, you have your mansion and you come home and you're alone; and here, if I come home, I can go out and there's people, and we're friends."

**Fuller and a young tenant play croquet.**

# 11

# AFTERWORD

I met Fuller and Kelly by chance, while researching *Common Ground*. I had called Art Gray, the photographer hired to shoot Millennium Santa Monica, and explained the focus of the book. He mentioned that he lived in the kind of multifamily housing I was interested in. Like me, Gray moved into his rental, the Third Street compound, thirty years ago and never budged, having found his domestic bliss. He invited me over, and before long I was quaffing drinks around the barbecue with Art and Tom and Bill. It was heaven. I was astounded that such an idyll existed, just three blocks from my own home. Like so many magical multifamily buildings in L.A. the Kelly/Fuller compound is concealed from the street. And so it is concealed from public appreciation.

This book started out as a quest: to make the case for multifamily housing in Los Angeles and to understand why it has occupied such a marginal place within the mythology of the region, despite the pleasures it can offer. Perhaps it is because of the hidden enchantment. Perhaps it is, to put it bluntly, because multifamily housing has been so stigmatized over a century of zoning, covenants, tax law, and mortgage lending practices, a stigma so deeply, culturally embedded that even many advocates of greater density still choose to reside in owner-occupied houses.

*Opposite: Neighbors sit around the fire pit at the 3rd Street Compound.*

And yet, there is a deepening awareness of a malaise in society—a malaise borne, perhaps, of hyper-individualism and intentional isolation which has divorced us from day-to-day neighborliness, its mutual dependency in all its comforts and irritations.

It is heartening to look back into the past and around the present to find many inspiring alternatives to the standard California dream. That dream—of owning a solo house in a yard under the sun, in the form of woodsy bungalows, grand villas in historic revival styles, or its supremely elegant Case Study Houses—has made living in Los Angeles a fantasy the world over. These homes went along with a twentieth-century experiment in living—independent, solitary, far-flung, reached only by car—which reached its apotheosis in the Los Angeles basin, a vast, undeveloped area that could be the canvas for an endless garden city. Yet while that radical experiment was underway, so too inventive builders and designers were testing modes of dwelling that offered up a counterpoint to this individualist lifestyle: socially centered dwellings that also deploy the architectural flourishes and innovations to be found in houses, from handcrafted revival styling through sliding walls of glass and, yes, the automobile. Because they were embedded in L.A.'s dispersed urban fabric, not dense city centers, these complexes became self-contained islands of coexistence. Secret places. Worlds within worlds. Common ground.

# Acknowledgments

It takes a village to realize a book about common ground. I am indebted to many people, starting with Paddy Calistro and Terri Accomazzo at Angel City Press. They supported the concept even when my narrative was unclear. Then Terri steered the manuscript into clarity with her extremely smart editing. J. Eric Lynxwiler made it sing with his graceful, bold design. For help with finding a voice, I am beyond grateful to Mattia Nuzzo, my wingman in the early stages of the project, when "multifamily housing in Los Angeles" seemed to be an impossibly vast topic. He unearthed buildings, pulled apart my copy, and insisted on a weekly meeting to check in on how the work was proceeding. His input was pivotal. Anastasia Tokmakova sorted out images with calm and humor, and she offered shrewd insights that also helped shape the story. Russell Brown has been a ceaseless cheerleader. Russell, and also Ric Abramson, Laura Chase, Todd Gish, Greg Goldin, Christopher Hawthorne, Steven Keylon, Barbara Lamprecht, Kathryn Smith, and Frederick Zimmerman read parts or all of the manuscript when it was near completion, and offered invaluable corrections and notes. Any errors are mine. Incidentally, Laura is the sister of the late John Chase, the wonderful writer, former urban designer for the city of West Hollywood, and beloved friend who inspired much of the thinking for *Common Ground*.

Thanks to all the photographers who allowed me to use their images that so effectively make the case for connected living in L.A. I extend special gratitude to Art Gray. He became a co-conspirator in the process, and took new photos of many of the buildings and their occupants that appear in these pages. Thanks also to all the archivists who provided vintage images, especially the staff at the Getty Research Institute for their patient support with repeated requests. The narrative would have had no beginning without aid from Lee Allen, Juan Dela Cruz, and John G. Ripley who were so generous with their expertise as well as amazing images of early bungalow courts in Pasadena. I am indebted of course to the scholars and journalists who have illuminated various aspects of multifamily living in Los Angeles, along with the many residents, architects, planners, builders, managers, and owners who shared their time and wisdom with me for site visits, phone interviews, and emails. In addition to those already cited in the book, I thank: Farooq Ameen, Emily Bills, Nathan Bishop, Lise Bornstein, Bill Bouchey, Madeleine Brand, Rene Buchanan, Cory Buckner, Claudia Carol, Winston Chappell, Mark Castellino, Joseph Coriaty, Joseph R. Coriaty, Ian Dickenson, Linda Dishman, Eve Epstein, Frank Escher, Aminatou Fall, Pedram Farashbandi, Anthony Fontenot, Chelsea Frank, Patrick Fredrickson, Bernard Friedman, Brent Gaisford, Joseph Giovannini, Marissa Gluck, Christine Goddard, Rebecca Greenwald, Frank Gruber, Ravi

Gunewardena, Eric Hemion, Kevin Henry, Delia Hitz, Alison Rose Jefferson, Nerin Kadribegovic, John Kamp, Gail Kennard, Michael Kesler, Brian Lane, Leonardo Lopez, Linda Lucks, Melissa L. Miller, Susan Morgan, Cindy Olnick, Daniel Ostroff, Bob Padgett, Matthew Parrent, Alan Pullman, Tash Rahbar, Stephanie Reich, Christian Robert, Erick Rodriquez, James Rojas, Diego Sagastume, Julie Silliman, Jeff Soler, Paul Solomon, Scott Strumwasser, Katrin Terstegen, Bobbye Tigerman, Michael Eisenstein, Patrick Tighe, Carolina Tombolesi, Barbara Turner, David Ulin, Evan Wilkes, Lyn Winter, Will Wright, Victoria Yust, Zoe Schweitzer, and Gary M. Zuckerbrod.

This book draws from years of collaborating with wonderful colleagues at KCRW on stories about housing and land use for *Which Way, LA?*, *Greater LA*, *Press Play*, and *DnA: Design and Architecture*. I am grateful to them all. Angela Anthony at Helms Bakery District has been a rock of support for the duration of this project, and working with her and Stephen Phillips on the 2021 exhibition *Low Rise, Mid Rise, High Rise* enriched my understanding of multifamily housing in L.A. I also honor the late Stephen Kanner, architect and friend, who first opened my eyes to the inspirational low-income courtyard housing built by Community Corporation of Santa Monica. But I may never have become so interested in apartments were it not for living in a lovely one. So of course I must thank the architects Frank Gehry and Fereydoon Ghaffari—and my great friend Julia Bloomfield, who introduced me to Frank back in the late 1980s. My dear parents, Eileen and Sam, sowed the first seed. They renovated houses and flats, and I and my sisters Nicolette and Isabel lived in each one as they remodeled, moving every two years or so. I often wished for a more stable home, but I came to cherish these adventures in residential space. My daughter Summer has had a very different childhood, having spent her entire life to date in one apartment building, and has shown tremendous patience in listening to me jabber about it even when she did not share my delight. My neighbors past and present—including Emmanuelle Bourlier, Fereydoon and Elizabeth Ghaffari, Hans Ghaffari, Marissa Fontana, Andreas and Nicolas Froech, Dilly and Aloka Gent, Jessica Himmel, Sharon and Steve Stein, Nicolas Weis and Juliette Jacqmin, Darlene Valentine—remind me by their presence why I love living here. Finally, there is my husband, Robin Bennett Stein, who urged me for years to write a book. I repeatedly said no, believing it to be too big a task. With his wind at my back, I committed to *Common Ground*, and I hope it fulfills the faith he has always put in me. I also hope it inspires him—a New Yorker and Europhile with limited love for Los Angeles—to appreciate the alternative version of the California Dream where we have had the good fortune to reside.

# Bibliography

"A Short Introduction to Zoning in Los Angeles." Abundant Housing LA, Sep 2, 2016.

Anderson, Michael H. *Urban Magic: Vibrant Black and Brown Communities Are Possible.* Los Angeles: Michael Anderson, 2021.

Architectural Resources Group. *Historic Context for Multi-Family Housing.* City of West Hollywood, (2008); "Garden Apartments of Los Angeles." LA Conservancy, October 2012.

Birnbaum, Charles A.. "The Village Green/ The Green Village." Village Green Owners Assoc., 2012.

"Bryson Apartments, Westlake, Los Angeles, CA." Pacific Coast Architecture Database, 2022

Buckner, Cory. *A. Quincy Jones.* London: Phaidon, 2002.

"Bungalow Courts in Pasadena." Planning and Community Development Department Website, City of Pasadena. Accessed Jul 18, 2022.

Chase, John. *Glitter Stucco & Dumpster Diving: Reflections on Building Production in the Vernacular City.* London: Verso, 2004.

Chase, Laura. "Gardens and Slums: House Courts and Bungalow Courts in Los Angeles, 1900–1930," n.d.

Cohen, Jean-Louis, Staffan Ahrenberg, and Ashley Simone. *Frank Gehry: Catalogue Raisonné of the Drawings.* Paris: Cahiers d'art, 2020.

Cuff, Dana. *The Provisional City: Los Angeles Stories of Architecture and Urbanism.* Cambridge, MA: MIT Press, 2000.

*CurbedLA*: Jenna Chandler. "You Can Now Buy a Piece of Echo Park for $100." Jun 5, 2020; Chris Eggertsen. "The Gorgeous Apartments That Became the Symbol of LA Noir." Dec 16, 2019; Hadley Meares. "The Story of the El Royale, LA's Most Glamorous Apartment Building." Jun 2, 2015; "Bungalow Courts Make the Best Neighbors." Jun 23, 2020; "The Dreams and Myths that Sold LA." May 24, 2018.

Divinity, Jeremy. "A Tale of Two Venices: Before There Was Dogtown, There Was Oakwood." *Knock LA*, Jul 9, 2020.

Falleta, Liz. "By-Right, By-Design: Housing Development Versus Housing Design in Los Angeles." New York: Routledge, 2020.

Fogelson, Robert M. *The Fragmented Metropolis: Los Angeles, 1850–1930.* Berkeley: Univ. of California Press, 1993.

Frampton, Kenneth. "The Usonian Legacy." *Architectural Review*, Dec 1987.

Gebhard, David, Robert Winter, Robert Inman, and Nathan Masters. *An Architectural Guidebook to Los Angeles.* Santa Monica, CA: Angel City Press, 2018.

Ghaffari, Fereydoon. *My Journey: From Anzali to Los Angeles.* CreateSpace Independent Publishing Platform, 2014.

Giovannini, Joseph. "Raising California: The architect Irving Gill infused the West with a spare modernity." *New York Times*, Mar 26, 2000.

Gish, Todd Douglas. "Building Los Angeles: Urban Housing in the Suburban Metropolis, 1900–1936," Unpublished Ph.D. dissertation, Dept. of Planning, Univ. of Southern California, 2007.

Goldberger, Paul. *Building Art: The Life and Work of Frank Gehry.* New York: Alfred A. Knopf, 2015.

Graham, Wade. *Dream Cities: Seven Urban Ideas that Shape the World.* New York: Harper Perennial, 2017.

Grant, Thurman, and Joshua G. Stein. *Dingbat 2.0: The Iconic Los Angeles Apartment as Projection of a Metropolis.* Los Angeles: DoppelHouse Press, 2016.

Greene, Robert. "Revising Los Angeles' DNA." *LA Weekly*, Apr 28, 2005.

Heskin, Allan David, and Jacqueline Leavitt. *The Hidden History of Housing Cooperatives.* Davis: Center for Cooperatives, Univ. of California, 1995.

Hines, Thomas S. *Richard Neutra and the Search for Modern Architecture: A Biography and History.* New York: Rizzoli, 2005.

Hopkins, Una Nixon. "A Picturesque Court of 30 Bungalows: A Community Idea for Women." *Ladies Home Journal*, Apr 1913.

"Housing as a Civil Right and Exclusionary Practices: The Way Forward." AIA Los Angeles.

Jefferson, Alison Rose. *Living the California Dream: African American Leisure Sites during the Jim Crow Era.* Lincoln: Univ. of Nebraska Press, 2020.

Kalish, Lil. *"For 50 Years, St. Elmo Village Has Been A Semi-Secret Creative Haven For Black Artists."* laist.com, Jul 10, 2019.

KCRW *DnA: Design and Architecture*: LA Designer: Patrick Tighe and John Mutlow Create "Architecture that Doesn't Discriminate" in West Hollywood, Mar 05, 2014; Skid Row Housing Trust Believes Good Design Can be a Cure, Jul 26, 20 Housing Crisis? A Pilot Project Has Some Answers. Jul 30, 2019; In an Age of Loneliness, Treehouse Offers Community

**Thanksgiving at Schindler House, 1924.**

That's Carefully Curated and Designed, Sep 23, 2020.

Kipen, David, ed. *Dear Los Angeles: The City in Diaries and Letters, 1542 to 2018.* New York: Modern Library, 2018.

Kries, Mateo, Müller Mathias, Daniel Niggli, Andreas Ruby, and Ilka Ruby. *Together!: The New Architecture of the Collective.* Weil am Rhein: Vitra Design Museum, 2017.

Kurtzleben, Danielle. "America's Yawning Racial Wealth Gap, Explained in 9 Charts." *Vox*, Feb 18, 2015.

Lindner, Diana. *Brave New Home: Our Future in Smarter, Simpler, Happier Housing.* New York: Bold Type Books, 2020.

Los Angeles City Planning: "Los Angeles Citywide Historic Context Statement," Dec 1, 2018.; "LA Multi Family Existing Conditions Analysis" Los Angeles City Planning, Jun 22, 2016.

*Los Angeles Times*: Lisa Boone. "They Turned a One-Car Garage into a Stunning ADU to House Their Parents. You Can Too." Oct 14, 2021.; Susan Freudenheim. "A Living Legacy Endures." Oct 16, 2002; Barbara Thornburg. "*Why Leave Home?*" Dec. 3, 2006.

Luckey, Gertrude Appleton. "Alexandra Court." *House Beautiful*, Nov 1916.

Marin, Rick. "Housing as Destiny on 'Melrose Place'." *New York Times*, Feb 11, 1999.

Matthew, Zoie. "How Community Land Trusts Could Make La More Affordable." *LAist*, Feb 2, 2021.

McCoy, Esther, and Susan Morgan. *Piecing Together Los Angeles: An Esther McCoy Reader.* Valencia, CA: East of Borneo Books, 2012.

McCoy, Esther. *Five California Architects.* Los Angeles: Reinhold Book Corp., 1960.

Nusbaum, Eric, *Stealing Home: Los Angeles, the Dodgers, and the Lives Caught in Between.* New York: PublicAffairs, 2021.

Parson, Donald Craig. *Making a Better World: Public Housing, the Red Scare, and the Direction of Modern Los Angeles.* Minneapolis: Univ. of Minnesota Press, 2005.

Parson, Donald Craig. *Public Los Angeles: A Private City's Activist Futures.* 45. Vol. 45. Geographies of Justice and Social Transformation Series. Athens: Univ. of Georgia Press, 2020.

Polyzoides, Stefanos, Roger Sherwood, and James Tice. *Courtyard Housing in Los Angeles: A Typological Analysis.* New York: Princeton Architectural Press, 1982.

Sherwood, Roger. *Modern Housing Prototypes.* Cambridge, MA.: Harvard Univ. Press, 2001.

Slater, Gene. *Freedom to Discriminate: How Realtors Conspired to Segregate Housing and Divide America.* Berkeley: Heyday, 2021.

Smith, Kathryn. *Schindler House.* Santa Monica, CA: Hennessey & Ingalls, 2010.

Stephens, Josh. *The Urban Mystique: Notes on California, Los Angeles, and Beyond.* Ventura, CA: Solimar Books, 2020.

Steverman, Ben. "Meet the Hipster Real Estate Developers Building for Millennials." *Bloomberg*, Sep 30, 2015.

Stuart, Carolyn. "Pueblo Del Sol." SAH Archipedia, Aug 5, 2020.

Vallianatos, Mark. "Forbidden City: How Los Angeles Banned Some of Its Most Popular Buildings." Urbanize Los Angeles Website, Sep 06, 2017.

Ventura, Anya. "The Rise and Fall of an American Dream." Getty (getty.edu), Jul 15, 2021.

Wallach, Ruth. *Los Angeles Residential Architecture: Modernism Meets Eclecticism.* Charleston, SC: History Press, 2015.

Webb, Michael. *Building Community: New Apartment Architecture.* London: Thames & Hudson, 2017.

Yorke, F.R.S., and Frederick Gibberd. *The Modern Flat.* London: Architectural Press, 1937.

Zeiger, Mimi. "Is Los Angeles a City of Houses?" MimiZeiger.com, Jun 14, 2016.

# *Index*

# Image Credits

The images in *Common Ground* are from the private collection of the author, except as noted below. The author and publisher thank the following sources and rights holders for permission to reproduce the images on the pages listed. Every effort has been made to properly credit the appropriate parties.

**Cynthia Alexandra**: 19, 162, 208, back cover • **Lois Arkin/LAEV**: 172 • **Artist Rights Society**: Fondation Le Corbusier, © F.L.C./ADAGP, Paris/Artists Rights Society (ARS), New York 2022: 102 (top) • **Caitlyn Atkinson**: 191, 192 • **Iwan Baan**: 116, 124 (left) • **Bestor Architecture**: 187 • **BRIDGE Housing**: 93 • **Brooks + Scarpa**: Photo by Jeff Durkin/Breadtruck Films, 114; photo by Tara Wucjik: 141 • **California State Library**: courtesy The California History Room, Sacramento: 58 • **Benny Chan**: © Benny Chan/fotoworks: 21, 117, 132 • **Clive Wilkinson Architects**: 152, 154 • **Cornell University Library**: Division of Rare and Manuscript Collections, Clarence Stein Papers, #3600, 101 **Cover**: photo by Emi Rose Kitawaki: 181 • **Juan Dela Cruz Collection**: 29 • **Paul Finegold**: photo © Charmaine David: 48, 52 • **Judy Fiskin**: 72 • **Getty Research Institute, Los Angeles (GRI)**: Special Collections © J. Paul Getty Trust:

Leonard Nadel Photographs, GRI (2002.M.42): 82 (right), 84, 86; Julius Shulman Photography Archive 1936–1997, GRI (2004.R.10): 14, 61, 73, 79, 88, 89, 97, 100, 138, 139; Frank Gehry Papers, © Frank O. Gehry, GRI (2017.M.66): 10; The John Lautner Archive, © The John Lautner Foundation, GRI (2007.M.13): 64 • **Art Gray**: 11, 16, 18, 22, 24, 36, 38, 40, 41, 47, 56, 80, 94, 96, 98, 108, 113, 131, 136, 137, 161, 166, 167, 168, 194, 195, 196, 207, front cover • **Tim Griffith**: 115 • **Gruen Associates**: 147, 148 • **Here and Now Agency**: 15, 145 • **Michael Kesler**: 37 • **KFA Architecture**: 142; photo © Jonathan Ramirez/ArchLenz Photography: 126 • **Lee Allen Family Collection**: 26 • **Nic Lehoux**: 134, 135 • **Library of Congress**: Historic American Buildings Survey (HABS): 45 • **LOHA**: Holos Communities (formerly Clifford Beers Housing): 125; photo © Lawrence Anderson: 129 • **Louisa Van Leer Architecture**: 183 • **Treehouse Hollywood**: photo by Tony Maesto: 165 • **Yoshihiro Makino**: 178, 180 • **Nico Marques**: 6, 176 • **Michael Maltzan Architecture, Inc.**: 156 • **Jonathan Moore**: 4 • **Moore Ruble Yudell**: photos by Colins Lozada: 122, 123 • **Neighborhood Investment Co. (Nico)**: 188 • **Omgivning/Studio-MLA**: 184 • **Jceal Parker**: 158 • **Rochester Institute of**

Technology **(RIT)**: Cary Graphic Design Archives, Alvin Lustig Papers, photo by Jay Connor: 74 • **Stephen Schauer**: 177 • **Kyungsub Shin**: 77 • **William Short**: 160 • **Southern California Library for Social Studies and Research**: California Eagle Photograph Collection, 82 (left); Housing Authority of the City of Los Angeles (HACLA) Photograph Collection: 90, 92 • **Eric Staudenmaier**: 27, 118, 120, 121, 149, 163, 174 • **Tim Street-Porter**: 34, 62, 146, 150, 151 • **Studio One Eleven**: 124 (right) • **Tighe Architecture**: photo by Bran Arifin: 2 • **UCLA, Charles E. Young Research Library, Dept. of Special Collections**: Richard and Dion Neutra Papers, 1925–1970, reproduced with permission from the Neutra Institute for Survival Through Design: 54, 60 • **University of California Santa Barbara, Special Collections**: Architecture and Design Collection/Art, Design & Architecture Museum: Irving John Gill papers, 42; R.M. Schindler Papers, 50, 201 • **University of Southern California Libraries, Special Collections**: California Historical Society Collection, 1860–1960: 30, 144; Edward H. Fickett, FAIA, Collection: 66, 67; Dick Whittington Photography Collection, 1924–1987: 102 (bottom) • **Joshua White/JWPictures**: 51 • **Kate Whitney-Schubb**: 45

**Opposite: The park by Formosa1140 draws neighbors and their dogs.**

Robin Bennett Stein

**Frances Anderton** covers Los Angeles design and architecture in print, podcasts, exhibitions, and at public events. For many years Anderton hosted *DnA: Design and Architecture*, broadcast on KCRW, a public radio station. Her honors include the Esther McCoy Award, bestowed by the USC Architectural Guild at USC School of Architecture, for her work in educating the public about architecture and urbanism.

Façade of Treehouse Hollywood, designed by TheCaliforniaOffice to encourage neighborliness.

*Common Ground: Multifamily Housing in Los Angeles*

By Frances Anderton / Copyright © 2022 Frances Anderton
Design by J. Eric Lynxwiler, Signpost Graphics

10 9 8 7 6 5 4 3 2 1    ISBN-13 978-1-62640-091-7

Library of Congress Cataloging-in-Publication Data is available

Published by Angel City Press, www.angelcitypress.com
Printed in Canada

ANGEL CITY PRESS